Published by Stormi Nelson

978-0-615-33068-6

Through the Core

Stormi Nelson

Table Of Contents

Preface..
I feel a lot of people don't understand homelesness has
a ripppling effect.

Unraveling................................
Life is much like a seam; one loose stich could lead
to all the work put into it...gone.

Injustice...................................
Not every homeless person resorts to stereotypical
activity.

Society...................................

You can loose the unspoken things in life that no
realizes they own.

Survival..................................
A key has a lot of in depth meaning to me; A person with
a key has a home, a car and a place to go.

Endurance..............................
I felt like I had been at war with my own country, and
I had the scars tprove it.

Giving Back..................................
I am survivor, that has gained an education no on could
ever teach; a lesson of life.

Advice
Work Citied

When I first started writing "Through the Core", I had no idea what my future held for me. My future held the same concept as my life at the time: unraveled, in pieces; some good, some bad.

My Mom was a big help through some of my darkest days. I can't imagine how much stress and worry she went through, and yet having the strength to help me. (Thank you Mom.).

I am grateful to so many people who have done more than I could have hoped for. Everyone who has helped me big or small gave me this compelling urge to write "Through the Core"; even if I had no clue what might come of it or any idea of which direction it might go. If did not mention you personally; I still appreciate everything and have not forgotten what you have done.

Just to name a few; I would first like to thank my Grandma Dangberg. Even in heaven, she is my foundation.

Next, I would like to thank Seneca Miller; she helped me find my first job after becoming homeless. She was always willing go beyond her job description in order to help; not just for me but for others as well.

Another person whom I am so blessed to have come into my life would be my angel who gave me my smile back. Even though I don't know her name, I am still touched by her generosity. Also, I thank her dentist who made it possible.

Shirley and Helen are two women who I am blessed to know and I am thankful to have them in my life.

A woman who always had a smile and a warm heart is Kara Barney. She was an important influence to me in the year 2004. She gave the advice to help me make it "Through the Core", and that is, no one can take my creativity from me. Everything else could be taken. I could allow someone to take it from me, by stop creating.

As long as I did not give up, I held one thing from my past that no one could touch. She was so correct!!! Through every blow I endured and remembered, I thought of what she said and kept creating.

I am grateful for Roberta and Elise from Pac-n Stor . Thank you both for coming into my life.

I hold so much gratitude for Avila Retail, without them this book would not exist. I send a big thanks to everyone at Avila Retail.

The most caring soul I have met been would be my friend, Matt. I would not be here today without him. Thank you for becoming a part of my family.

I owe a debt of gratitude to three more people who made publishing this book possible. I would like to thank Carrie and her daughter for allowing me to have a place to finish this book. I could not finish writing my story without their neighbor who I have come to call "Miracle Mario". Thank you all so very much.

Greg, I thank you for all of your help along with the heartache and obstacles you have placed in my life. My life definitely would not be the same without you in it.

I thank all of you, who shared yourselves through stories, pictures or in other ways. I hope one day everyone who is homeless could make it through the core.

One last person I would like to mention is Billy Owens. He is someone who has been a great support and wanted so much to be a part of my story. For everything he has done for me, and all the times he made me laugh when all I wanted to do was cry I wanted to grant his wish.

You see them everywhere. Dirty and disgusting probably would come to your mind, as your eyes glance through a homeless person on the street. I can't imagine you actually seen him or her; at least without dehumanizing him or her. Do not feel guilty; most I believe; judge and condemn the invisible.

I walked in both shoes. I shamefully admit harbouring judgmental eyes; until I traded shoes with the man I judged.

I never imagined owning or walking in a homeless man's shoes, but I don't regret what life taught me.

> *This is my story, our story...*
> *Maybe yours one day,*
> *But I'd hope not;*
> *Take a Walk with Me;*
> *Through The Core.*

Forget not who I am;
For our paths may have crossed;
Nay'r look down upon me;
For you may walk in my shoes.

A stranger;
Doth have friendly eyes;
Walk hand in hand with me;
Get to know me,
And enemies we wilt be no more.

Stormi
2005

No one should have to beg for food in one of the richest countries in the world.

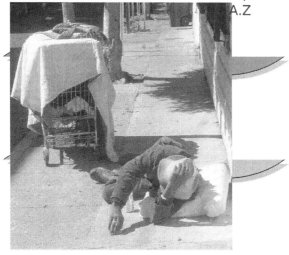

(O.G. & Al) Phoenix, A.Z

PREFACE

Late one afternoon I decided to drive to Pac N Stor where my belongings were stored at. My reflection in the rear view mirror catches my eye. While being held up by rush hour traffic, I turn the mirror to get a better look at myself. My auburn hair shimmers as the sunlight dances across my head. A sparkle from my barrette made me notice how long my hair has grown. It was well past my shoulders now. I pull my sunglasses down my nose a bit to check my make-up. The eye shadow I chose accented my hazel eyes perfectly. My blush I applied was just enough color on my pale skin to bring out my high cheekbones.

Looking at me today one probably would never believe that I once lived on the streets. With a single glance, a stranger would probably never presuppose that I am a survivor of homelessness.

Slowly the traffic starts to moves again so I return the mirror back to its correct position. One of my favorite songs is playing on my car stereo. I reach down to turn it up and tap my fingers to the beat on my steering wheel.

A sense of relief and compassion swept through me as I notice a man digging in a trash can at a bus stop. The gentleman did not accidentally throw something. He was obviously digging for something to help him survive that day. My heart ached for him as I thought about how fortunate I was. I wondered how many people were affected by his downfall.

I feel a lot of people don't understand that homelessness has a rippling effect. When someone becomes homeless the whole family is affected in some way. Whether it is less contact with that person or the pressure of wanting to help; everyone involved with that person's life can experience the after math of homelessness. Even miles apart the rippling effect can touch the lives of those who love and care about the person who has been displaced.

Even the individuals who don't have family in this world. You don't have to be related to someone to touch someone's life in some way, and your's affect theirs.

If you cannot imagine yourself as being homeless imagine someone close to you going through such drama. Visualize for a moment that suddenly life and routine are torn apart completely. There is no closure to anything especially relationships. In your mind can you sense what impact these circumstances would have upon you?

As for myself, the idea or thought of moving was never even considered. Nothing was packed or stored in order to be unpacked in a new place. When I was forced to move I was unprepared for the situation which led to the inevitable fact of losing everything.

I am not sure of all the lives my displacement may have touched of all the people who knew me.. I believe my Mom felt the homeless ripple the most out. Just like most mothers who doted over their children my mother was the same. I can only speculate as to the overwhelming anxiety she that must have experienced.

She had no idea what she could do to help, yet she desperately wanted to. We lived miles and miles apart from one another so she could only imagine what I had to be dealing with.

Living in a small town in the Midwest most of her life sheltered her from the actual reality of homelessness can cause and the devastation of it. The only knowledge she had about homelessness was from the television. It grieves me to this day to imagine what turmoil she must have felt and the sheer hell of not knowing if I was alive or dead.

Another thought to ponder over if you are homeless; who would you ask for help. Would you want to burden your family or friends with your own problems?

I have never built a close relationship with anyone in my family due to growing up in a broken home. I had a lot of family I could have contacted for help if I would have found their phone numbers. Even if I had those phone numbers; I believe I would have remained in Phoenix. It felt awkward to ask for help while not being close on a personal level. [1]

---

1 The next pages contain thoughts from a man in Florida

Many homeless people have separated themselves from whatever family they had for their own reasons. While some well meaning people may try to make them get back together, it's not something for others to decide for them. People outside the family may not realize what's involved. Making a person go back to where they will be ridiculed doesn't help them get their life back together.

Most homeless people may have parents, a parent, perhaps many brothers and sisters or children. Even so they remain homeless on the street, struggling to just exist. Why then don't they go to the family members and get some assistance?

Many homeless men have wives, or ex-wives, and children which they are not allowed to see. Even so they may be expected to pay child support. If they work and make some money, most of it is taken away. Some have their drivers licenses revoked too for not making child-care payments, making it even harder to make enough to even support themselves.

I have seen people, apparently family, yelling and swearing at each other in public and feel very glad that I don't have to even live near them. Many people live in homes where there is constant fighting and hostility. Being homeless is extremely difficult but not necessarily as bad as living in some homes.

Two guys who were brothers once invited me to stay with them. After visiting and listening to about an hour of their drunken yelling I walked out and went back to my camp in the woods. There is no way I could possibly live like they did. **(HomelessAmerca.com)**

Today I am grateful for the small things in life. I know the truth about being homeless. I have survived and understand how easy it is to lose everything. I know everything can disappear in a blink of an eye and never to return. Through survival on the streets, I know how difficult it is to come back. Struggling with life on the streets was the most difficult role in my life. Homelessness is a title that I pray to never carry again. I feel for those who carry that title today. I wish someday everyone who has become homeless; will be blessed with some good fortune in life.

Homeless holds a new meaning for me. Having nothing means just that, nothing. No position in society, no civil rights, no voice; a loneliness no words can describe is all that most own but cannot express. I was once trapped in that world and that is why I speak out today. I hope if anything I can be the voice of someone who cannot be heard.

I know that the only way we can help the homeless is to push past the stereo types. We as a society need to stop the judgmental thinking in order to listen to the cries from those in need. I don't know if there can ever realistically be an end to homelessness, but I do know us as a society could put an end to the suffering for a lot of homeless individuals and families. I fully believe if we as a nation would put half as much energy into saving our own people as we do to saving the rest of the world we could possibly help millions.

The traffic slows to a crawl as I approach an on ramp congested with rush hour traffic. I tilt my head back to relax and allow my mind to digress back to the year 2002. I start to think about my life right before I became homeless.

I was a different person then. I was so dependent upon my husband for solving everyday problems. I could not imagine allowing someone so much control over my life as I had back then. My whole world revolved around my husband's needs and wants. I put him and everyone else above my own desire in life. I made myself unimportant.

For years I watched my husband, Joe, my friend, my confident, slowly disappear. I didn't want to believe or imagine he was slowly fading away from me. Nor could I envision he would take me to the brink of insanity.

Slowly I watched the man I knew immerse into a stranger; lost to himself, to everyone, and anyone; including me. I hoped, prayed, begged, and bartered for his return. Only a glimpse of the man I knew would show now and then. Sadly, the man I loved and was devoted to would never return to me. I will always love and miss that man who disappeared long before he physically left.

I put up with so much abuse and neglect from him; always hoping he would come back. I never wanted to give up on him. I thought somehow he would recover. I wanted to believe he was just dealing with something he would have to think about while finding a solution to whatever was troubling him. At the very least, I hoped it was all a phase.... maybe a mid-life crisis. As much as I wanted to believe one of those situations to be true, I realize now, I was very wrong.

Instead, he slipped further and deeper into insanity. The farther he drifted the more I would try to reach him. Pain and conflict was my only reward for my effort. As I think back: I suffered more than I could ever imagine and utter words for.

Looking back I know now; that love and trust were my first two nails in my coffin; to becoming homeless. I believe we can all be guilty of those qualities. Usually those qualities in a person are considered good. So over all; I feel my first two mistakes were not errors; only circumstance.

First I want you to understand, the man I married, was much different from the man he became. The man with curly red hair and bright blue eyes was a brilliant person that was quick on his feet. He was well built but gentle as a kitten. He was so thoughtful and caring. He was always very protective toward his family.

The person I imagined spending the rest of my life with was part of me; my soul mate. He was my right arm, and my life functioned as such. A decision I formed unconsciously; made it so nothing in my world functioned correctly without him.

For instance; I never took the time or concern to ascertain my way around; even in the city I called home. I always let him guide us. He knew how to get to our destination. Joe never was confused by directions so I relied and trusted him to navigate. Looking back I can see I became to secure. I never stopped and thought about needing to know the information myself. I always counted on him to be there.

I trusted his judgment over mine. I looked up to him as my hero. He would always give me my creative space any artist craves. He would even be supportive at most of my crazy new hobbies. He'd always be just far enough away to be able catch me if I fell. I guess I saw him as my fairy tale knight; who rode upon a white horse.

I counted on him to always be there somewhere. Even when we would have to be separated from one another, I knew he was there in the shadows. He was a military man and separation was a familiar routine in our life. Neither one of us was jealous towards the other. We both knew where our hearts stood. Loyalty towards our relationship was strong in both of us. We both felt an unbreakable bond when we were first married. Trust at times is all we had to build a relationship upon.

Like most military men, I've come to know, he worked hard; not only at work but at life as well. It was easy to allow him to make most of our decisions financially and legally. He took the lead at paying our bills. I never thought to question who or what he would be spending our money on. He planned well for our future. I felt secure and safe from our arrangement. Every day he would bring home a smile and sometimes a surprise. Whether it was flowers or a simple note to remind me how much I was loved I treasured and craved the gesture from him.

Like me, he was old fashioned in many ways. He was the open door type of gentle man. He wouldn't leave me behind; no matter what situation occurred. If I could not be included; he would not include himself and I returned the same concept towards him.

We were equals. Our lives were entwined into one functioning unit. We both had contributing functions in our relationship; which made us like one whole person, I guess. He paid the bills, I bought groceries; for example. Today I do both and can't imagine how or why I didn't do the same before; I feel we still would have been equal.

Anyhow, that was the man I married. He was everything to me, my world ...my happiness. He came into me life like a lamb and left like a lion.

I don't know exactly when He started to disappear, but my guess would be around the time he was released from the military. We both suffered finical setbacks when he left the military.

He was in the military for ten years. At the time it was known as the ten year mark. The military had too many people enlisted during his career and many people including Joe were more or less forced to leave the military.

We were both unemployed and falling behind in bills fast. I lost my job from an injury at work that labeled me as permanently, partially disabled. We lost our townhouse and moved into an RV with the help from my Mom. Joe took all that very personally. He was a proud man and not being able to support us made him depressed. Like I said he was old fashioned in many ways.

I would console him; by trying to convince him, we could get through our set back. I fully believed we could get back a lifestyle we once shared. A life that would be finical stabile; consisting of plans to reach futuristic goals. I felt he wanted the same as I did. I believed in so much it blinded me from the truth

He became distant, and withdrawn. He was so silent, angry, and bitter. Maybe he blamed me but never said it aloud; I know I will never know for sure.

I understand we all change as we grow or age in this world, but how Joe changed was a bit abnormal.

It is hard to imagine seeing someone struggle upon daily habits, such as getting dressed. I find it unbelievable myself. To this day I wonder what was happening to him, because whatever was going on inside his head; was obviously not in his control.

I would literally have to tell him every step for him to accomplish a simple task of putting his shirt on or putting on his shoes, just to name a few things,

I would, for example, say, "Put your arm in your sleeve. Now the other one.... Okay now, button the bottom button and the next one."

He would get annoyed and so would I, truthfully. I'd leave believing he should not need help on such repetitive life doldrums. Really, how many countless hours do we spend dressing ourselves?

Moments later; much to my surprise, I would see him stuck in his world, and not have getting any farther from when I left him.

His world; as I came to call it; consisted of staring blankly at whatever would be in front of him, and or rocking side to side whether he was standing or sitting. If I could get him to respond, much of what he said never made sense to me. Usually, what he said would not pertain to the conversation at the time.

I'm sure his view of his world was much different than how I saw it. There were days I felt as though he were in a snow globe; unreachable, yet visible, and easily shaken. Those days; I wish I could see what he saw; maybe I would understand him then or at least relate to his thoughts. I began to mourn for the hidden truth that lies; behind the agony of insanity.

For some reason I watched him struggle, yet hoped for the same result from him as when he was normal. Looking back, I can't believe I expected such.

Some days he would be the man I knew. I'd always silently rejoice. I felt so thankful hoping we could finally move forward together again. Unfortunately, he would again disappear, drifting a step further from me. He slowly became a stranger that I believe even he would not know.

Being in the military, he didn't know where to start. The military, programs the soldiers to follow the orders given to them. Even the leaders follow orders. After ten years of following orders, a situation like ours must have been overwhelming. I wish I realized this concept when we were experiencing it, but everything does happen for a reason.

Days turn to months; months to years; I focused on each day as problems arose. I never planned for a future; at the time, there was no future. I became greatly ill myself. I was so sick that sometimes just breathing was an accomplishment. I pushed my pain aside. I was not worried about myself. My only concern was for a future and us together again. My energy was focused on doing everything in my power to bring my husband back to me. I never thought I was sick enough to see a doctor. The thought of why I was ill or I could die never did not enter my mind. Nor did I realize how isolated I was and how helpless that could make someone.

Eventually his silent anger snapped into abuse. He became both verbally and physically abusive. Why did I stay?

Today, I don't hold a logical answer. At the time, I excused it as insanity. I still believe the madness inside him made him violent, but no longer excuse it.

I feel several reasons subconsciously held me there. For one thing, abuse has been very much a part of my life. As a child, I have suffered physical, mental, verbal, and sexual abuse. Like most of generation-x, I came from a very broken family. I learned to adapt and be accepted by pleasing people. As child, I would do all I could most of the time to make others comfortable and happy. Other peoples' pleasure became my own happiness. I never knew what I liked or really wanted. I lived to serve.

I learned to fend for myself in order to survive but I never thought for myself. I never learned how to think only of myself.

When I became sick especially the last year and a half we were together; I know now that focusing on me was something I never knew. I always considered I had a cold or the flu. I didn't stop and consider how often I was sick and who or what could cause it. I never saw a pattern to my illness until I was no longer with Joe.

I dealt with the headaches, nausea, and vomiting as I came down with them. I learned that I would have this incredible hunger like pains. They were odd sort of pain; not quite hunger pains but yet hard to explain.

I would put off eating as long as I could because I knew what would follow. Eating anything would set off the vomiting which made my stomach cramp up so much that curling up into a ball would be the only way for some relief.

A fever would quickly set in; it would be so high that I would become delusional. I remember many times of dreaming or thinking about water. I would become so thirsty; yet too weak and having delusions to get a drink for myself.

Dehydration I believe caused my muscles to cramp and ache. Sometimes just stretching an arm or leg would contort my muscles into a Charlie horse. I would be sick like this for three to four days, but it sometimes took up to a couple more days to be strong enough to walk without falling. I wasn't sick like this just once or even twice but so much that I could not begin to guess how many times I was sick.

Each time I wrote it off as the flu or a bug of some sort; I didn't assume to be ill again. Who does? When I was sick; I would be too ill to take myself to any hospital or doctor. I would be bed ridden and alone. Yes, I said alone.

Where was my husband? Your guess would as good as mine. He would leave on some excursion to a friend's house. Never do I recall him asking how I was nor worrying. He would stay away until I found him.

Where did my hero go? I didn't want to believe he could be doing this to me and still don't want to. I do know as think back that this became like a sick and demented game. I would become sick and he would disappear,

Years later I would discover through hair analysis that the reason I was sick so often in the year 2002 was due to being poisoned. All signs point to him for my demise. I can't believe or say that it is true. I will admit though; since he has been gone from my life; I have never become sick like that again.

My appearance of once having a yellowish skin tone and hair falling out in clumps has again become more human looking. I use to suffer from weird chemical burn like rashes. My skin would literally have bubbly hot boils like someone threw hot water on me. That too has never resurfaced.

I still don't feel like the most beautiful person, but I feel I look good enough to be seen again. When I was ill I felt like the hunchback of Notradame; I too wanted to hide in a church tower.

I had so many chances to save myself. There were so many red flags that my world and life were crumbling. Denial blinded my confidence and self-pride drove me into believing I alone could fix the problems in my marriage.

I never saw it coming until it was too late. I never realized how close to the edge I was, until that final blow towards my life in society. I fought to keep myself from slipping down to where "the scum" of society lives. On February 14, 2003; I lost that battle; by then it was too late to turn back.

When the reality surged through every fiber of my body; no sound could I utter. I just collapsed upon the ground; hoping I would wake up safe in my own bed.

In my head I was silently screaming, "Where did I go wrong? Please God rewind this insanity and give me one more chance; I know I would do everything right. Not me; I'm helpless and there is no one. No one cares. I'M INVISIBLE!!"

And when I could finally stand; that thought of invisibility, became my reality. I quickly realized; I wasn't alone; I had only felt that way.[2]

---

2 Our country's homeless are on the rise and other countries have noticed this. The next few pages are from an article in

Pictured: The credit crunch tent city which has returned to haunt America

By <u>Paul Thompson</u> Last updated at 12:35 PM on 06th March 2009

A century and a half ago it was at the centre of the Californian gold rush, with hopeful prospectors pitching their tents along the banks of the American River.

Today, tents are once again springing up in the city of Sacramento. But this time it is for people with no hope and no prospects.

With America's economy in freefall and its housing market in crisis, California's state capital has become home to a tented city for the dispossessed.

Rich and poor: The tents and other makeshift homes have sprung up in the shadow of Sacramento's skyscrapers

Europe.

Shanty town: The tent city is already home to dozens of people, many left without jobs because of the credit crunch

Those who have lost their jobs and homes and have nowhere else to go are constructing makeshift shelters on the site, which covers several acres.

As many as 50 people a week are turning up and the authorities estimate that the tent city is now home to more than 1,200 people.

In a state more known for its fantastic wealth and the glitz and glamour of Hollywood, the images have shocked many Americans.

Conditions are primitive, with no water supply or proper sanitation. Many residents have to walk up to three miles to buy bottled water from petrol stations or convenience stores.

Ben Cardwell, carries supplies to his tent at a homeless settlement

Tammy Day, a homeless woman, cooks potatoes on a campfire at the site

At other times, charity workers arrive to hand out free food and other supplies.

Joan Burke, who campaigns on behalf of the homeless, said the images of Americans living in tents would shock many.

'It should be an eye- opener for everybody,' she said. 'But we shouldn't just be shocked, we should take action to change things, because it's unacceptable.

'It is unacceptable that in this day and age we have gone back to a situation like we had during the Great Depression.'

Homeless: Keith and Tammy Day cook dinner

Authorities in Sacramento, where Governor Arnold Schwarzenegger has his office,

admit the sight of families living in such poverty is not pretty.

But faced with their own budget crisis and a £30billion deficit, they have had little choice but to consider making the tent city a permanent fixture.

The city's mayor Kevin Johnson said: 'I can't say tent cities are the answer to the homeless population in Sacramento, but I think it's one of the many things that should be considered and looked at.'

Shanty towns sprung up during the Great Depression as people lost their jobs and homes

Migrant **Mother: Dorothea Lange's famous photograph from the Great Depression Features Florence Owens Thompson, 32, a mother-of-three who had just sold the family's tent to buy food**

As America's most powerful state California had the same gross domestic output as Italy and Spain, but it has been among the hardest hit by the recession and housing crisis.

Foreclosure rates last year rocketed by 327 per cent, with up to 500 people a day losing their home.

Coupled with massive job cuts that have seen one in ten workers laid off, many people who once enjoyed a middle class existence are now forced into third world conditions.

Former car salesman Corvin and his wife Tena are among the newest residents of the tent city.

Tent city residents queue up to receive supplies handed out by a local charity

The couple, who are in their fifties, lost their home and jobs around the same time.

With homeless shelters full in Sacramento, they had little choice but to use what savings they had left to buy a tent.

The couple admit they have yet to tell their grown-up children about their hand-to-mouth existence.

Tena said: 'I have a 35-year-old son, and he doesn't know. I call him, about once a month and on holidays, to let him know that I'm well and healthy.

'He would love me anyway, but I don't want to worry him.'

The shame of Sacramento's tent city was given a much wider airing after it was featured on the Oprah Winfrey show which is watched by more than 40million people a week.

Many of those who have found themselves homeless worked in the building trade.

But with no new home builds and as many as 80,000
people losing their job every month, there is little chance of
employment. Governor Schwarzenegger last month approved a
budget to address the state's deficit, ending a three-month stalemate
among lawmakers.

As well as increasing taxes, he has imposed drastic cuts in
education, healthcare and services that will affect everyone living in
the state.

Many of those living in the tent city are pinning their hopes
on President Obama's $787billion stimulus package which is aimed
at rescuing the economy and creating jobs.

The President has also announced plans to save the homes
of nine million people from foreclosure by restructuring their
mortgage debt.

(Thompson, Pictured, 2009)

Chapter One

UNRAVELING

Homelessness results from a complex set of
circumstances that require people to choose between
food, shelter, and other basic needs. Only a concerted
effort to ensure jobs that pay a living wage, adequate
support for those who cannot work, affordable housing,
and access to health care will bring an end to homeless

. Reference: (Homeless) Fact Sheet #1

I find it amazing how fast goals, dreams, and planning of life can unravel. I found life to be much like a seam; one loose stitch could lead to all the work put into it gone. One could stop the process but to prevent one thread becoming loose is nearly impossible.

Most take precautions in life to be prepared for sickness, retirement, and other things like fire or theft. We buy false sense of security through insurance and benefits. Almost everyone, I would bet believes they would never really have to use such security or find themselves needing more.

About one week after Thanksgiving 2002, I found myself in desperate need of any help available. A knock on my Winnebago door would soon change my life, my world, and my hopes of a future with Joe.

As innocent as it sounded that knock could have been the death bell. The park manager stood on the other side of the door; she might as well have been the grim reaper because the news she brought abruptly ended my life, as I knew it.

At the time, I did not know that the life I was living would never again come to life. The life I had lived, the person I grew up to be, and the dreams I desired all died that day. One knock, simple, ordinary, and a daily occurrence; who could imagine; it could hold such an impact.

According to the park manager, Joe had not paid the rent like he said he had. We were months behind and now asked to leave the park. We held a lease with the park and we should have been allowed a normal eviction process. The park manager would not allow any time for us to try to start the Winnebago ourselves; instead they forcibly towed the Winnebago.

The Winnebago started and drove fine. Why the park insisted on towing us out of the park is beyond my understanding. I always thought we were towed for humiliation. Having us towed out seemed and felt like it was entertaining to everyone in the park.

Maybe I saw things incorrectly but I know my feelings will never change.

I cannot forget how the residents in the park gathered to watch as though it was a ticketed event. Their laughter and cheers will be forever in my memories.

And to add to our consternation not only did anyone refuse to help they stole whatever they felt they needed or desired. It was very obvious to me that we were not welcomed in that park.

I now know that how we were removed from the park is illegal. At the time I knew nothing of rental agreements, or renters' rights and Joe, well he was not any help. In the end, we were towed out.

We had been living in that park for a few years by then so our Winnebago was skirted. Underneath the Winnebago had become storage. We had accumulated a lot of stuff over the years living at the park. We were towed over and through everything underneath. I was not allowed any time to move anything. They didn't unplug the electric or disconnect the sewer hose; both made the back wall tare loose.

I couldn't watch any more without doing something so I did the only thing I could think of at the time. I dove under my Winnebago and crawled to the middle where I would be unreachable. The dual tires prevented anyone big, and inflexible to grab me. My plan worked. They stopped towing and asked me to get out.

"Not until you at least disconnect the Winnebago properly", I yelled from under my Winnebago.

The manager and assistant manager did in fact attempt to grab me by reaching under the Winnie. I saw an arm come towards me on one side of the Winnebago. I avoided contact by sliding to the other side a bit. Another hand came towards me from the opposite side and I avoided it by doing the same thing. After a bit, the arms stopped reaching under the Winnie. I could see their legs and feet gather into a huddle. For a moment, it was silent.

"You have to move or you will be run over", I heard someone say, in frustration, breaking the silence.

A small crowd was gathering by then, and I replied towards the crowd "You are all witnesses, if they run me over, it is attempted murder."

With that said; the crowd became more of a group. The park manger did unplug the Winnebago. I then relented and gave up. As much as I hated to, I crawled back out from my hiding place so they could finish towing the Winnebago out of the park.

After the park manager released the Winnebago back over to Joe and I that night; we became transitionally homeless. I never understood that term. To me a person is either homeless or not homeless. How could anyone be in between? I thought of myself as not homeless but instead address less.

My life was now turned upside down. I had no clue on what to do next. I had no one to turn to for help. Little did I realize at the time I was on a sinking ship and the best thing I could have done was bail out. I have always been stubborn and determined to never give up. At the time; that determination blinded me from seeing the truth. I pushed on by believing a better future was in sight.

Stopping the Winnebago was a problem. Several years before our brakes had gone out. We never had them repaired because we had parked and made it a home. If and when we plan to drive it again we planned only then to have the brakes fixed. We never thought about sudden circumstances.

Not having any brakes was only an obstacle for us; we adapted and came up with a crazy solution. I replaced the brake with a cement block. Now, I know you are all probably wondering how can one stop a moving ton vehicle with a cement block. With a little determination and a lot of luck it is possible.

The process of stopping took a bit of work and skill. I simply rode ahead of the Winnebago on a push scooter while carrying a cement brick. I would then drop it where the Winnie needed to stop by kicking it off of the scooter with my foot.

There was only one time that idea almost backfired. I placed the brick too far away from the front tire so I dropped the scooter and pushed it with my foot.

The Winnie was moving quickly towards me and I had pushed it too far. It was too late to do anything so I turned my head and closed my eyes as I realized it was going to run me over. I knew it would hit my leg or ankle. I chose to have my leg crushed hoping it would be easier to fix.

Much to my surprise nothing happened. I opened my eyes to see that Winnebago had come to a stop by hitting the curb. The front wheel was just touching my leg. I must have had an angel on my shoulders that day, and I was very thankful for it.

We quickly realized that there are laws about parking a vehicle on the streets of Phoenix. Our Winnebago suddenly became too big. It was thirty-two foot long. I always felt the need for more space until I had to find a place to park it. About every two or three days we would move it to another location. Due to the stopping situation we never moved it too far. We would move it just enough that anyone could see that it had changed locations; sometimes it would be just around the block.

A few police officers in the area found our routine annoying. They chose to harass us instead of pointing us in a direction where we could maybe receive some type of assistance. It quickly became a day to day battle with the law. The police wanted our Winnebago off the streets and we refused to become homeless.

At least for myself I was not going down without a fight. Everything I owned was at risk. Every memory, every photo, keepsake, and future hope was at stake. I was not about to just walk away from that. It was my life and who I grew up to be. What I had left might not have been important to an outsider but for me it was all I had and all that I knew.

I do admit that our Winnebago was a bit of an eye sore to most. It was older, a bit worn and the back wall was loose. Most of the stuff we stored underneath I put on the roof and covered it with a tarp.

I had no idea on what else I could have done. I was hoping to be able to get to a storage place. In order to store our processions; we either had to have the brakes fixed or find someone with a truck. I thought between the two of us; getting our stuff into a storage unit should not be hard. I quickly comprehended that I was once again on my own.

My goal was to get the Winnebago back into an RV park. It was only weeks from Christmas and the snow birds had every available spot filled. I knew I had to wait them out until after Christmas.

I did not know what I was getting myself into. Today, knowing what I know now; I would have left all that I had owned in Phoenix, and moved back to my family in Nebraska. The decision to stay in Arizona; was my first step into the core.

The Winnebago I owned; was originally, a book mobile. It looked like a very large cargo van when I first bought it. I had to put in a couple of year's worth of construction; before it was worth living in. I liked the fact that it had no windows because I was able to keep it cool during the hot summer days in Arizona.

Since the Winnebago had only a windshield and no other source for light; it was very dark inside at any time of the day. My solution to that problem was candles. I had candles burning at all hours of the day. I would burn about twelve small pillar style candles a day.

I thought I was careful. I always put them inside candle holders so the candles would not tip over. I never knew that some type of candle holders can start on fire.

One night, about two weeks before Christmas in 2002, our Winnie was parked behind a Taco Bell in a church parking lot. I was sound to sleep on the sofa when a voice screamed at me to get up. I opened my eyes and saw a wall of fire about two to three feet high! Popping and crackling sounds could be heard as the fire hungrily consumed our processions. It grew larger by the seconds. Looking around I quickly realized I was surrounded by glowing orange. I was trapped; both doors were blocked by fire.

For some reason I was not afraid or bothered by the thick black smoke. I couldn't see anything but the fire; everything else was black. The heat was intense but I ignored it. Something or someone was obviously watching over me and somehow I knew what I needed to do.

My only hope was through the ceiling hatch that luckily Joe and I had put in several years ago. We thought ahead about such things as fire so we had a few escape routes put in. I never thought I would actually have to use them.

I very calmly reached up through the smoke, found the hatch and pushed. The hatch did not budge. I tried to force it open by pounding on it. Again the hatch did not move. I was not alarmed just determined to open the hatch. My guardian angel was not only protecting me from the fire but from panic as well.

Joe happened to be on the roof and heard me pounding on the hatch. He managed to get it open by using his pocket knife. The next thing I knew I was engulfed by fire. When Joe opened the hatch; the fire went up, over, and through the opening. I assume, somehow, I had survived a back draft.

My fingers were burned from the fire ball. All the hair on my arms was gone. Some of my hair on head was also singed.

Joe was also touched by the fire. Both of his arms and his face looked kind of like a sun burn. We were both very fortunate to not have been hurt more than that.

Fear overwhelmed me when I understood finally that it was amazing I was alive at all. I realize I probably should never have wakened. The burns on some of my fingers were causing me unbearable pain. The cold night air felt like daggers so I tried to cover them with my end of my sweater I was wearing. The warmth of covering them hurt just as much so I decided to hold my hands close enough to me so the wind would not feel like a knife slicing at the burns.

The fire ball that came from our roof drew enough attention that someone called the fire dept. Before I could take in what was happening flashing lights from the Phoenix fire department caught my eye.

Joe had somehow managed to put the fire out by then so they focused on me. All of them were amazed that I had no smoke inflammation. Other than the burns, the only evidence that I was trapped inside was the smoke damage on the clothes I was wearing.

When I owned the Winnebago I experienced one problem after another. There never was a dull moment in my life. Everyday seemed as though some type of drama was going on around me.

About two weeks before Christmas we were parked in back of a Lutheran Church in Phoenix. That afternoon; I heard a knock, on my door. I thought maybe someone was bringing a little holiday cheer. I was shocked to discover that the person knocking on my door had little idea of what the true meaning of Christmas was.

"You have to move your Winnebago", grumbled a white haired gentleman, "You are ruining our Christmas Festivities."

I was dumb founded, but I didn't argue or become belligerent. I simply said as nice as I could, "Okay, no problem. I will move it as soon as possible."

I was frustrated. I wanted to ask if they knew what Christmas was really about. Did they have a clue what it stood for? Had that church ever heard of Christian charity? As much as I wanted to ask those questions I kept them in my thoughts and began to ponder where I could park during Christmas.

That Christmas would be the last holiday I would spend with Joe. I don't think I will ever forget that melancholy day. Most of the day I stayed in the Winnebago; thinking, hoping, and planning for the following Christmas.

"Next year will be better," I said solemnly.

Joe didn't say anything. He didn't have to. His piercing blue eyes held a disdain sadness that told what he was thinking. I could see he was holding back the misery we both felt.

Days earlier I had found a bunch of illuminating Christmas angels. Instead of moping and wishing for a better holiday; we decided to change our mood by spreading a little holiday cheer. We placed an angel in a box; one for every person had treated as unethically in the past few months.

Before heading out that Christmas Eve; Joe helped me treat my injured hands. We then both changed in two dress attire. Then we blew out the candles; crawled out onto the roof hatch and down the ladder, into the damp evening air. Joe put his arm over my shoulder and pulled me close to him. I placed my head on his shoulder and we started to walk towards the last church that we had been parked at.

We walked inside the church and located the office. Joe knocked on the door, and patted a few wrinkles from his dress pants.

Seconds later the door opened. We immediately recognized the gentleman as the person who claimed that we were ruining his festivities. His expression upon seeing us was a sort of bewildered look of surprise.

"We just wanted to wish you a merry Christmas," Joe said with a smile; breaking the odd silence.

"And to thank you," I added as I took an angel from the box and handed it to him.

By the time we had delivered the last angel we had tears in a eyes from laughing. The expressions we received and the loss for words mumbles; was humorous to us. As I crawled back inside the Winnebago that night; my heart and soul felt at peace; from showing true meaning of Christmas to those who had more but seemed to have forgotten.

A dark cloud seemed to have settled over us. If there was a possibility of something to wrong it did. Our declining relationship and arguments in the trailer park had involved the police. The city had filed charges against him on one occasion which had placed him on probation. Not having an address is considered a probation violation.

About one week after Christmas, Joe and I were at a friend's house. The phoenix police knew he was there, and arrested Joe on a warrant for probation violation. He was sentenced to six months in prison.

I had no idea at the time have to write him. We also had no address for him to write me back I was left to wonder how and if; we would ever find each other again. I was left with an overwhelming situation to face on my own.

I only knew two people in Phoenix. I had no idea where anything was located. If it was not on a map; I could not find it. I only knew how to get to a few places; all of which were located about five blocks or less from the trailer park that we had lived at.

Getting lost when you're driving is frustrating, but getting lost when you are walking is a daunting frustration I cannot describe to you. I don't think the words exist to describe how overwhelming it feels.

The year 2002 ended without me celebrating it. I stayed in my Winnebago and hoped the following year would be better. At the time I was still planning for future that would never exist.

Unknown to me, that New Year's Eve, I would see Joe one last time the following year. That last moment would be brief and at a friend's house that he happened to stop by to inquire about me. I would; just happen to have been there. He would then disappear back into the dark Phoenix night and out of my life forever.

I had to adapt to my limitations and learn to adapt to my forever changing surroundings. I knew nothing about Phoenix; including the law, the people, and the city in general. All of which left me vulnerable to a wide variety of problems.

Do to being homeless I felt that society had labeled me as a nuisance and a menace. Asking for directions or for help of any type;

I found to be impossible at the time. American Society; hold onto so many stereo types and misconceptions about homeless people.

3

Panhandlers Are Homeless

It's a common conception that if you see someone panhandling (begging) that they must be homeless. Actually, most panhandlers are not homeless.

For many it's just an easy way to get money, possibly for drugs. Most panhandlers have somewhere to live, and some live very well. Of the homeless I have been familiar with, very few will panhandle regularly. Some will when they haven't been able to make any money on day-labor jobs for a while, and then just to get a few bucks. There are those who panhandle as a profession, making over a hundred dollars a day, and therefore don't have to live on the street.

I saw one article that stated that 90% of the homeless [in that city] panhandled. That's an easy conclusion if you make the assumption that all the panhandlers you see are homeless. I may see two panhandlers a day, while there are thousands of homeless in the area where I live. Most homeless people don't degrade themselves by begging.

Charities have had to turn away more people in recent years. Where I live there isn't shelter space for even 10% of those in need.

3   The next few pages are a list of stereotypes that the homeless are labeled with. If you are homeless or become homeless; American Society will classify you in one or more of the following stereotypes.

Simply getting shoes to wear is difficult. It' not unusual either for local city governments to come up with new restrictions aimed at closing down soup-kitchens and other assistance specifically to run the homeless out of town (and into someone else's jurisdiction).

As for food stamps; (which you must qualify for by seeking work and doing public service). If a person works even part-time it may disqualify them from any assistance, even though they still can't even afford a rental room.

They should be put in Mental Institutions.

It's true that perhaps a third of homeless people have some type of mental problems, some significant enough to prevent them from maintaining jobs or dealing with life situations. Many do get help on an outpatient basis but still can't afford housing or maintain work. Legally, only those who are a threat to themselves or others can be forced into mental care institutions. The days when anyone acting strange was locked up are long over. Many homeless who have significant physical or mental problems still get nothing in government assistance. Many have been turned down so many times that they have given up all hope

.It's their own fault.

It's true that many people are homeless as a result of making wrong choices in life, but many have problems, such as with health, that they did not cause. How many people choose to get cancer or arthritis? A substantial percentage of the working U.S. population is only a couple paychecks away from being homeless, and that percentage is increasing. How many people make a deliberate choice to be homeless?

Homeless people are criminals.

The rate of serious crime by the homeless is not much different than the general population. It's true that many homeless frequently face time in the county jail due to minor violations such as open-intoxicants, trespassing, and so on. Most serious drug addicts have money and homes. Do you really think the multi-billion dollar drug trade in the U.S. is funded by homeless people? If the media

covers a crime and the accused is homeless, they make sure to point
that out in the headlines. When a homeless person is assaulted, even
to the point of having to be hospitalized, and robbed it usually
doesn't even get a paragraph in the paper.

All they need to do is get a job.

Just getting a job won't get anyone off the street.
Maintaining a job that pays enough to afford housing and other
living expenses is what is necessary. Being without housing, clean
clothes, transportation, food, and other necessities makes it nearly
impossible to become established long enough to maintain any kind
of meaningful work.

Homeless people steal shopping carts. *I occasionally see a
homeless person on the street with a shopping cart, and some of
these are old rusty one from stores that don't exist anymore. Most of
the time it's lazy people taking their groceries home, after which they
abandon the cart. When you see shopping carts left in front of homes
and apartments it's not the homeless. It's just irresponsible people
that don't care. I saw dozens of carts abandoned at one expensive
apartment complex.*

Homeless people get all their medical care for free.

It's true that if anyone who goes into an emergency room with a
potentially life-threatening problem, they will get medical attention.
It doesn't matter if they are homeless or wealthy, a tax-paying citizen
or illegal alien. There are some local government agencies that
provide limited medical assistance for those who can clearly not
afford it. This is for low income as well as homeless people. If a
person has a problem such as partial paralysis or severe back pain
which prevents them from working they are unlikely to get anything
more than some cheap over-the-counter pain pills. Even if surgery
could correct the problem for a few thousand dollars, there is no
assistance. The person may eventually be able to get on disability,
but nothing to correct the problem. The government would rather pay

out hundreds of thousands in disability checks than correct the

problem for a few thousand and have the person go back to work.[4]

(HomelessAmerca.com)

---

4 after reading a homeless man's view I feel that the
next article about unnecessary laws toward the
extremely poor and homeless becomes more logical

By BARBARA EHRENREICH

Published: August 8, 2009

IT'S too bad so many people are falling into poverty at a time when it's almost illegal to be poor. You won't be arrested for shopping in a Dollar Store, but if you are truly, deeply, in-the-streets poor, you're well advised not to engage in any of the biological necessities of life — like sitting, sleeping, lying down or loitering. City officials boast that there is nothing discriminatory about the ordinances that afflict the destitute, most of which go back to the dawn of gentrification in the '80s and '90s. "If you're lying on a sidewalk, whether you're homeless or a millionaire, you're in violation of the ordinance," a city attorney in St. Petersburg, Fla., said in June, echoing Anatole France's immortal observation that "the law, in its majestic equality, forbids the rich as well as the poor to sleep under bridges."

In defiance of all reason and compassion, the criminalization of poverty has actually been intensifying as the recession generates ever more poverty. So concludes a new study from the National Law Center on Homelessness and Poverty, which found that the number of ordinances against the publicly poor has been rising since 2006, along with ticketing and arrests for more "neutral" infractions like jaywalking, littering or carrying an open container of alcohol.

The report lists America's 10 "meanest" cities — the largest of which are Honolulu, Los Angeles and San Francisco — but new contestants are springing up every day. The City Council in Grand Junction, Colo., has been considering a ban on begging, and at the end of June, Tempe, Ariz., carried out a four-day crackdown on the indigent. How do you know when someone is indigent? As a Las Vegas statute puts it, "An indigent person is a person whom a reasonable ordinary person would believe to be entitled to apply for or receive" public assistance.

That could be me before the blow-drying and eyeliner, and it's definitely Al Szekely at any time of day. A grizzled 62-year-old, he inhabits a wheelchair and is often found on G Street in Washington — the city that is ultimately responsible for the bullet he took in the spine in Fu Bai, Vietnam, in 1972. He had been enjoying the luxury of an indoor bed until last December, when the police swept through the shelter in the middle of the night looking for men with outstanding warrants.

It turned out that Mr. Szekely, who is an ordained minister and does not drink, do drugs or curse in front of ladies, did indeed have a warrant — for not appearing in court to face a charge of "criminal trespassing" (for sleeping on a sidewalk in a Washington suburb). So he was dragged out of the shelter and put in jail. "Can you imagine?" asked Eric Sheptock, the homeless advocate (himself a shelter resident) who introduced me to Mr. Szekely. "They arrested a homeless man in a shelter for being homeless."

The viciousness of the official animus toward the indigent can be breathtaking. A few years ago, a group called Food Not Bombs started handing out free vegan food to hungry people in public parks around the nation. A number of cities, led by Las Vegas, passed ordinances forbidding the sharing of food with the indigent in public places, and several members of the group were arrested. A federal judge just overturned the anti-sharing law in Orlando, Fla., but the city is appealing. And now Middletown, Conn., is cracking down on food sharing. If poverty tends to criminalize people, it is also true that criminalization inexorably impoverishes them. Scott Lovell, another homeless man I interviewed in Washington, earned his record by committing a significant crime — by participating in the armed robbery of a steakhouse when he was 15. Although Mr. Lovell dresses and speaks more like a summer tourist from Ohio than a felon, his criminal record has made it extremely difficult for him to find a job.

For Al Szekely, the arrest for trespassing meant a further descent down the circles of hell. While in jail, he lost his slot in the shelter and now sleeps outside the Verizon Center sports arena, where the big problem, in addition to the security guards, is mosquitoes. His stick-thin arms are covered with pink crusty sores, which he treats with a regimen of frantic scratching.

For the not-yet-homeless, there are two main paths to criminalization — one involving debt, and the other skin color. Anyone of any color or pre-recession financial status can fall into debt, and although we pride ourselves on the abolition of debtors' prison, in at least one state, Texas, people who can't afford to pay their traffic fines may be made to "sit out their tickets" in jail.

Often the path to legal trouble begins when one of your creditors has a court issue a summons for you, which you fail to honor for one reason or another. (Maybe your address has changed or you never received it.) Now you're in contempt of court. Or suppose you miss a payment and, before you realize it, your car insurance lapses; then you're stopped for something like a broken headlight. Depending on the state, you may have your car impounded or face a steep fine — again, exposing you to a possible summons. "There's just no end to it once the cycle starts," said Robert Solomon of Yale Law School. "It just keeps accelerating."

By far the most reliable way to be criminalized by poverty is to have the wrong-color skin. Indignation runs high when a celebrity professor encounters racial profiling, but for decades whole communities have been effectively "profiled" for the suspicious combination of being both dark-skinned and poor, thanks to the "broken windows" or "zero tolerance" theory of policing popularized by Rudy Giuliani, when he was mayor of New York City, and his police chief William Bratton.

Flick a cigarette in a heavily patrolled community of color and you're littering; wear the wrong color T-shirt and you're displaying gang allegiance. Just strolling around in a dodgy neighborhood can mark you as a potential suspect, according to "Let's Get Free: A Hip-Hop Theory of Justice," an eye-opening new book by Paul Butler, a former federal prosecutor in Washington. If you seem at all evasive, which I suppose is like looking "overly anxious" in an airport, Mr. Butler writes, the police "can force you to stop just to investigate why you don't want to talk to them." And don't get grumpy about it or you could be "resisting arrest."

There's no minimum age for being sucked into what the Children's Defense Fund calls "the cradle-to-prison pipeline." In New York City, a teenager caught in public housing without an ID — say, while visiting a friend or relative — can be charged with criminal trespassing and wind up in juvenile detention, Mishi Faruqee, the director of youth justice programs for the Children's Defense Fund of New York, told me. In just the past few months, a growing number of cities have taken to ticketing and sometimes handcuffing teenagers found on the streets during school hours.

In Los Angeles, the fine for truancy is $250; in Dallas, it can be as much as $500 — crushing amounts for people living near the poverty level. According to the Los Angeles Bus Riders Union, an advocacy group, 12,000 students were ticketed for truancy in 2008.

Why does the Bus Riders Union care? Because it estimates that 80 percent of the "truants," especially those who are black or Latino, are merely late for school, thanks to the way that over-filled buses whiz by them without stopping. I met people in Los Angeles who told me they keep their children home if there's the slightest chance of their being late. It's an ingenious anti-truancy policy that discourages parents from sending their youngsters to school.

The pattern is to curtail financing for services that might help the poor while ramping up law enforcement: starve school and public transportation budgets, then make truancy illegal. Shut down public housing, then make it a crime to be homeless. Be sure to harass street vendors when there are few other opportunities for employment. The experience of the poor, and especially poor minorities, comes to resemble that of a rat in a cage scrambling to avoid erratically administered electric shocks.

And if you should make the mistake of trying to escape via a brief marijuana-induced high, it's "gotcha" all over again, because that of course is illegal too. One result is our staggering level of incarceration, the highest in the world. Today the same

*number of Americans — 2.3 million — reside in prison as in public
housing.*

*Meanwhile, the public housing that remains has become
ever more prisonlike, with residents subjected to drug testing and
random police sweeps. The safety net, or what's left of it, has been
transformed into a dragnet.*

*Some of the community organizers I've talked to around
the country think they know why "zero tolerance" policing has
ratcheted up since the recession began. Leonardo Vilchis of the
Union de Vecinos, a community organization in Los Angeles,
suspects that "poor people have become a source of revenue" for
recession-starved cities, and that the police can always find a
violation leading to a fine. If so, this is a singularly demented fundraising strategy. At a Congressional hearing in June, the president of
the National Association of Criminal Defense Lawyers testified about
the pervasive "over criminalization of crimes that are not a risk to
public safety," like sleeping in a cardboard box or jumping
turnstiles, which leads to expensively clogged courts and prisons.*

*A Pew Center study released in March found states
spending a record $51.7 billion on corrections, an amount that the
center judged, with an excess of moderation, to be "too much."*

*But will it be enough — the collision of rising prison
populations that we can't afford and the criminalization of poverty —
to force us to break the mad cycle of poverty and punishment? With
the number of people in poverty increasing (some estimates suggest
it's up to 45 million to 50 million, from 37 million in 2007) several
states are beginning to ease up on the criminalization of poverty —
for example, by sending drug offenders to treatment rather than jail,
shortening probation and reducing the number of people locked up
for technical violations like missed court appointments. But others
are tightening the screws: not only increasing the number of
"crimes" but also charging prisoners for their room and board —
assuring that they'll be released with potentially criminalizing levels
of debt.*

Maybe we can't afford the measures that would begin to alleviate America's growing poverty — affordable housing, good schools, reliable public transportation and so forth. I would argue otherwise, but for now I'd be content with a consensus that, if we can't afford to truly help the poor, neither can we afford to go on tormenting them.

Barbara Ehrenreich is the author, most recently, of "This Land Is Their Land: Reports From a Divided Nat

(Ehrenreich, 2009)

INJUSTICE

*People who have no choice but to be
homeless have no choice but to be in public. To punish
them for this; heaps injustice on top of indignity. As one
Santa Monica woman who is homeless wondered,
"When does it stop? Are we going to push people off
the face of the earth? I do have a right to exist. I have
the right to food, clothing, and shelter because I live."*

*Thousands of citations have been issued
nationwide. Police continuously misapply and
selectively enforce existing laws in order to harass
people who are homeless and move them from parks to
neighborhood to alleys and back into parks. This
strategy demonizes poor people and feeds negative
public sentiment to target people who experience
homelessness, rather than root causes of homelessness
itself.*

Reference: (nationalhomeless.org)

How does one survive on the streets? Would you know how to find food or shelter? Could you survive if you had nothing? Have you ever thought about such concepts when seeing or a place to sleep that night? No longer are daily doldrums taken for granted when a person is homeless. There is no down time to enjoy the norm. The luxury of personal refuge is gone. I found places to accompany personal hygiene issues.

I quickly discovered grocery stores, gas stations, and a couple of apartment complexes with single public bathrooms. As long as I was fast, I could lock myself in a public bathroom; clean up and change my clothes before anyone would notice. I never took up to much time because I knew a paying customer could complain to a manager about the door being locked. I would always clean up any mess that I had made so no one would assume someone used their facilities as a personal bathroom.

I realized that if anyone caught on to my idea; I would most likely, be considered a nuisance and for that reason I would go to a different place almost every day. After I ran out of places; I would then go back to the first place, then I would go to the second location, and so on. By doing that, I would only use a place about every three or four days. Not every homeless person resorts to stereotypical criminal activity. **Ann and Charles** pictured here were

hard at work washing car windows at a gas station in Phoenix. Like me they too were determined to earn a living even if it was only for tips from the understanding of strangers. Society's' attitude should commend people like Ann and Charles instead of condemning them for their efforts.

Now that the economy's crashing, it turns out

I've been out there gathering valuable tips for millions of new paupers. And let me clarify, I'm talking real poverty. . That's the kind of poverty a lot of people are going to be experiencing soon -- and I'm here to tell you, it can happen here and it can happen to you.
(unnomunous)

As for myself, I learned to be resourceful. I was not able to gain employment so I figured out how to be an entrepreneur. I never begged or asked for money on street corners. I worked hard and made money by dumpster diving. That job, I learned is not as easy as it sounds. That job was one of the most physically demanding jobs I have ever done. It also was one of the most hazardous and stressful. The setbacks did not stop me. I was determined to earn my way back into society.

There is a technique to dumpster diving. I learned quickly that some dumpsters are not worth looking in. Yet, some dumpsters are worth looking in every night. I had found several dumpsters worth checking every night. Those locations became a nightly routine I called "rounds" mostly because they made a circle.

I chose places where I knew I could find new or gently used items. I would then clean them, and or fix anything that needed to be done to get in order for it to sell. I would then package or repackage the product before selling it at park and swap. Even though what I sold was considered trash; I would never sell junk. Everything I sold was new or looked new. I wanted to be respected as a vendor. I did not want anyone to purchase merchandise from me out of pity. I don't think my customers knew I was homeless when I was a vendor in Phoenix.

I never did and still don't feel guilty selling merchandise that someone considered trash. The reason I don't is because I look at goodwill and thrift stores merchants of society's trash. The products they sell have been disregarded by someone. The only difference between a thrift store and me was I had to locate my merchandise instead of it being donated.

I found a creative way of selling small things that wouldn't sell alone. For example, small items like travel soaps and lotions sell better together than separate. Through trial and error, I figured out how to put together gift baskets! I learned I could sell a travel shampoo for about a quarter but placed into a gift basket I could easily get five dollars or more.

I would sell on the weekends and during the week I searched for merchandise to sell. On Friday evening, I would pack the bike cart I owned. I then would prepare the long haul to park and swap by making sure everything was properly tied down and my bike was in working order. I had a unique bike cart made out of a garden cart. That cart could hold a lot of weight so I would get as much stuff to Park and swap as someone with a small pickup.

I was camping out about three miles away from park and swap. It was a long and tiring hall mostly uphill to park and swap. There were times my bike cart was so heavy that I would have to get off my bike in order to turn it. The weight made it nearly impossible for me to peddle my bike normally. I would push down with one leg and then back peddle. In order to rest one leg I would switch legs now and then.

What could possibly be found of value in the trash? You would be amazed. Behind stores new items any one could imagine can be found. In video rental dumpsters; movies are tossed out.

In fact, a dumpster dive behind a Blockbuster helped me off of the streets for a couple of months. One night on my route I found so many Vhs tapes that I got tired of picking them up! There were hundreds of movies. Now before you all head out to your nearest video dumpster; I want to say I was in the right place at the right time, and not every night is like that. I just happen to hit that dumpster when Blockbuster decided to change over to Dvd. It was just blessed luck and nothing more

Little did I know; I was breaking a law in Arizona. Dumpster diving is illegal and punishable by a fine up to two hundred dollars and or jail time. The law is supposedly to help identity theft, which is ludicrous. If anyone would actually think about that idea and seriously wanted to keep identity theft down a law of not shredding evidence would be more likely to make sense.

The only other excuse I have heard for such a law is dumpster divers make a mess. The business owners seem to have an odd fear of trash being thrown everywhere. I understand I can only speak for myself, but everyone I knew including myself would clean up after herself or himself. In fact, I have been known to leave a place cleaner than when I came. No one bites the hand that feeds it. Almost anyone can comprehend, that if you wish to return, then don't make the owner not want you be there. Something else for everyone to think about is: if you face the possibility of jail for dumpster diving like you could for shoplifting, why go through all the hassle of digging in the trash?

Dumpster diving is hard work. It is hazardous to one's health. Have you ever really looked in a trashcan? I believe most of the dumpsters could turn one's stomach just by the smell alone. So like I just pointed out why would anyone want to dumpster dive if you faced the same punishment as shoplifting? If I knew I faced jail for dumpster diving I think I would have resorted to criminal activity.

I feel having laws for minuet things in life could make actual crimes more appealing. If you own a business wouldn't rather someone, take your trash than your merchandise? In my opinion, I feel that arresting people for taking trash is a waste of taxpayer's money. Why should we pay someone to watch trashcans? Isn't there enough actual crime in this world to keep our police force busy?[5]

---

5 The next page contains tips from an unknown homeless person and the National Coalition for the Homeless about being prepared for the worst.

Planning for Homelessness

Think there might be a spell of homelessness in your future? Here are some things you need to consider right now! Denial: Don't do it. If you are close to becoming homeless you will be riding an emotional rollercoaster. The worst thing you can do is go into denial about what's coming. The best thing you can do is start to plan. Here are some considerations for those facing the awful step into homelessness. The suggestions here are for those without a car but many are viable for both situations.

1. Shelter: Buy a tent, an air mattress, a foot pump, ground cloth and a large backpack. It's best to buy a camouflage tent that blends in with woods.

2. Begin looking for a patch of woods near a bus stop to pitch your tent. Be at least 50 yards off the road. Don't share your campsite with others. Your stuff might not be there someday when you return. Pay attention to getting located near a water point, a business where you can fill jugs with drinking water. Look for a faucet on the side of convenience stores. You will probably have to look toward the outskirts of town but being close to a bus stop is important. check nearby businesses to see if their bathrooms have electrical outlets where you can plug in a set of clippers. A sheet is a good idea. On hot summer nights you can soak it in water to cool you down and help you get to sleep. (This is from someone I knew who was homeless for a while).

3. Set aside 2 changes of clothes and a jacket and raincoat, buy some sunscreen, a hat, nail clippers, first aid ointment, band aids and bandages, pens, paper, LED flashlight, gallon plastic bags for keeping things waterproof, scissors, pocket knife, table knife, fork and spoon, plastic plate and electric clippers for cutting your own hair. You will need a pot and pan for cooking.

4. Get a library card if you don't have one. You can job hunt on the computers there and check out books as well. And they have air conditioning which is nice in the summer months.

5. Get a Post Office box if you don't have one. You need somewhere you can get mail. You can use general delivery if you want but it's better to have a box.

6. If you haven't already apply for food stamps and unemployment. Use your Post Office box to receive mail. Check the yellow pages for charities and get their phone number and address.

7. You won't be able to move all that you need to your campsite in 1 move but with 2 or 3 trips you should have enough to be at least semi-comfortable. **(unnomunous)**[6]

Things to Do if You May Become Homeless in a Few Days

If you only have a few days before you may become homeless, it is helpful to start making plans. The goal should be either to avoid going to an emergency shelter, or, if that can't be avoided, to make your stay there as short as possible. Depending on how much time you have before you might become homeless, try one or all of the following:

1. Try to locate an assistance program near you.

Some agencies provide homeless prevention assistance. These programs may have waiting lists, require an appointment/interview, or have certain restrictions on who they serve. For these reasons, the sooner you can find a program that may be able help you, the better. If you do not know of any programs near you, the section Sources of Help may help you find one.

2. Apply for Public Housing and/or Section 8 Housing

Waiting lists for public and Section 8 housing vary across the country, but in many cases, the waiting list for public housing is shorter than for Section 8 housing. You can find out how to apply by looking for the number of your local public housing authority in the government section of the phone book.

3. Apply for Transitional Housing

In some communities, transitional housing is an option for people who are homeless. Transitional housing programs vary greatly across the country as far as who they serve and what their requirements are. You will have to fill out an application and make an appointment for an interview. Follow through with as many of these programs as possible.

4. Make sure your ID is current and available.

If your driver's license has expired, or been taken for a traffic ticket, etc., reapply or get your State ID processed. If you only have a printout of your Social Security Card, get a new card to replace it as soon as possible. Many shelters and employers have strict ID requirements, and it will make things easier if you have these things ready or in process. Set up a P.O. Box for delivery and mail if that is possible.

5. Make an Emergency Pack.

If you have more than two bags for yourself, or one for each child, try to find someone you know who can and will hold your things for you. Almost every shelter has limits on the amount of baggage people can carry with them because they don't have enough space.

Pack the things you can take with you. Try to arrange a ride or some sort of transportation for the day you'll have to leave. If there is anyone who can lend you some money, now would be the time to borrow it. Try to keep at least $20-$50 with you in a safe place just for emergencies. Make sure your ID is in a safe and accessible place -- you will want to take it with you.

Some shelters charge money, or have strict ID requirements. These recommendations are just suggestions so that you will have the most resources at your disposal when you need it.

(Homeless, 2

The next few pages consist of another homeless man's opinion to consider.)

Attempting to Work While Homeless

In the viewpoint of many people the solution to all homelessness is for people to simply "get a job". That sounds simple and easy, just get a job. In the real world however, getting and maintaining a job to afford housing while homeless is hardly that simple.

For those with homes, cars, good clothing, phones, and all the typical necessities of everyday life it can still be difficult to find, and keep, employment that actually pays a good living wage. When a person has none of these things maintaining meaningful employment is a hundred times more difficult. Getting a job is hard enough, keeping the job requires much more. There are several factors in maintaining a job. Those who have never been without any of the basic necessities can easily assume that everyone has access to them.

Adequate Sleep

Having to sleep on the ground and dealing with rain, thunderstorms, oppressive heat or freezing cold, mosquitoes, and night foraging animals can make it difficult or impossible at times. Add to that the very real danger of being attacked, robbed, beaten, or even killed, and then try to get some sleep. Working close to others demands good hygiene. Not being able to even shower frequently, or have clean clothes, rules out any employment like this.

Imagine using plastic to try to stay warm and dry

Keeping Clean

Any indoor work demands being clean and outdoor labor work requires being able to clean up afterward. Sleeping outside in your clothes doesn't help. Some places provide showers for the homeless, but due to location and time they are unavailable to most in need. Getting appropriate clean clothes is a major problem. When clothes get dirty and wet they stay that way. Few places will help people with washing clothes for free.

A Place for Belongings

Keeping a supply of clean clothes and personal items is extremely difficult while living outside. If your things are stolen or vandalized (often burned) it's considered to be your own fault for not having housing. Carrying everything around (even if that were possible) doesn't help in maintaining a "normal" appearance.

Transportation

Relatively few homeless; have cars, or can afford to keep them running. This leaves the bus system, bicycles, or walking. Some areas have good bus systems, but they don't always go where the jobs are. With waiting, transfers, plus walking it can take hours. A trip that takes 20 minutes by car can take two hours or more by bus.

You would think that bus systems could get people to jobs early in the morning. The bus system where I live (PSTA in Pinellas County FL) is fairly good, but most buses don't run early enough for a person to get to a 7AM job, even if the bus runs on schedule.

I live close to Tampa, Florida, and there are work opportunities there and a bus system. So, why don't I use it? I live in another county, which has it's own bus system, but there is no connection from here for the regular buses. The two bus systems could cooperate, but they don't, so you simply can't get from one to the other.

Communication

How can an employer reach a homeless person who applied for work? Being without a mailing address or phone number makes it very difficult. If a temporary agency needs someone for an opening they choose from those they can reach immediately. Most employers will not even consider anyone who doesn't provide a phone number.

Conflicts with the Law (or the Community)

Police generally don't bother people sleeping outside unless it's private property or visible to the public. With public pressure on authorities to eliminate the homeless it keeps getting more difficult. I've been stopped by police repeatedly just for walking to work early in the morning. "Normal" people don't walk to work in the morning when it's still dark.

Undue Suspicions

While some employers may be understanding, and even flexible on terms, knowing that a person is homeless, most are not. If you don't show evidence of a place to live people automatically assume you're a criminal. If you don't have a drivers license they assume that it must have been revoked for drunk driving, or some offense. Many employers won't
consider anyone using a shelter as an address (even if it is discrimination). Many homeless people don't have any significant job or personal references either.

Food

Until that first paycheck, which could be weeks, you still need to eat. There are some places that provide free lunches or dinners for the homeless but, especially for those trying to work, may be inaccessible due to time of day or location. Some soup-kitchens have been forced to close as a means of "eliminating the homeless". I know of one mission that had been serving free breakfast and dinner to anyone coming in for about 20 years that was ordered by the city to stop providing meals on the grounds that they didn't have adequate parking. Most of the people coming there didn't have vehicles, but it was a convenient way of stopping them from helping people. Many churches provide free groceries, but it doesn't help a lot with nowhere to cook, or even store any food. .

The Cost of Housing

With minimum wage work, even if it's full time, it's difficult to rent even the cheapest rooms and then afford other necessities like food. Renting an apartment may require putting $1000 down (if not far more) plus proving adequate wages to qualify. The cost of housing has been going up much faster than wages in much of the country. A good job requires
having housing and affording your own housing requires a job.

Competition

Even for some of the hardest, dirtiest, and dangerous low paying jobs there is competition. It's not unusual to have dozens of applicants for one job opening, and employers don't choose based on the person's need.

Some may think that a homeless person can just go to a public shelter and get all the help they need. In reality, even if the local area has a shelter it's probably full to capacity. If a person is fortunate enough to get in, they are likely limited to only a few nights. Even then,
the shelter isn't responsible to provide any further assistance that may be needed. Could you get a job and save enough to rent a room simply by having a bed and a shower for a few nights?

There are some unavoidable facts to all this. Being able to get, and maintain, a job which will pay enough to make it possible to get permanent housing usually requires having housing and other assistance to get started. Without some kind of assistance unemployed
homeless people are likely to stay that way, no matter how hard they try on their own.

Having Proper Identification

With increased government controls on acquiring identification, like state I.D. and birth certificates, it's harder to get your own papers even if you were born in the US. In order to get a copy of your own birth certificate you have to show proof of identification, and to get identification, you need a birth certificate. For many people, it can take months of government red tape just to prove they are an American citizen. If you can't get any identification you can't work, even if you were born in the United States and have lived here all your life. If your wallet with your I.D. is stolen you have to start all over again, as if you were an illegal immigrant.

Driving a taxi in urban areas is among the most dangerous jobs, yet
many people with skills for far better paying jobs still do it as a last resort.

Comments, suggestions, or questions?
email me at:clyde@homelessamerican.com (**HomelessAmerca.com**)

One incredible incident of injustice I lived through would be the first week of February 2003. For about a week, due to being broke down, the Winnebago had been parked at a Baptist church on the eastside of Phoenix.

I was no longer allowed on the property; due to being parked at the church's parking lot longer than the pastor had wanted me to park there. Somehow, I had to move my Winnie off that property even though I could not be on the property myself. Another stipulation that added to my demise was the fact that only I could drive the Winnebago (at least according to what the police told me).

I never understood what anyone was trying to accomplish by wanting me to abide by those rules. I owned an RV (Recreation Vehicle) not an RC (Remote Control). If I did not have to abide by those restrictions I would have had the Winnebago moved within a couple of days from the first time the minister had asked for me to move it.

One week had gone by since I devised a plan with a friend, to work on the Winnebago at night. As the sun rose, I would go across the street and sit in the shade in front of an apartment complex. I wanted to be close enough to watch my home so nothing would happen to it.

This plan worked for the first few days and my Winnebago was just about fixed. My friend and I made a crucial mistake before we had it able to start. That mistake was pushing ourselves to hard which caused us both to fall asleep.

The sun was up when we awoke, and I was well aware it was too late to be able to leave without being seen. My friend left since he didn't have a trespassing warrant placed upon him. I believed I would be safer if I stayed put.

I watched him climb out onto the roof, and heard the familiar sound of the ladder being lowered. The sound of his footsteps soon followed and then I heard him place the ladder under the Winnebago.

I was alone with only my nerves for company. Every sound I heard was so eerie and loud. My Winnebago had no windows, so I could only imagine what was going on outside. The sounds I heard toyed with my imagination and added more stress upon myself.

Most of the noise was from the wind or traffic. The sounds of people just outside of my home made me nervous. I knew I was the topic of conversation, but I could not understand what exactly what was being said. I wanted to believe I was safe even though I felt trapped.

I lay back on my sofa and tried to relax. I could hear people talking and walking outside close to my Winnebago. After a while, the voices faded and I heard whoever was outside walk away.

Finally, it was silent outside. I closed my eyes thinking I was protected in my home. A short time later, I heard a familiar sound of a tow truck.

In a panic, immediately my mind began racing through ideas of what to do. (Do I go out or stay inside?) Feeling like I had no choice; I climbed out of the safety of my home. I knew my Winnebago could not be towed if someone was inside.

Much to my surprise the driver showed interest only in me. I could hear him on his cell phone.

"Yeah, I see her," he said into the phone, "Can't tell; maybe five foot something. No brown hair. She is wearing…"

I had heard of crazy stories about law enforcement, but until then I never experienced anything that I had read or heard about. I believed the articles that I had to be just stories. I knew in a heartbeat this was not a typical tow truck driver, but an undercover officer instead.

I needed to get off that roof and fast. I looked around for a way down since my ladder was gone.

Jump instantly went through my head. I went to the side, looked down, and knew this was not an option. Fourteen feet is not high unless you happen to be looking down.

The driver caught on to what I was trying to do as he watched me look for an option off my roof, and yelled out, "Stay put, my supervisor is coming, and he wants to talk to you."

"Stay put," I mocked him under my breath like I would have done to my one of my siblings' years before. My gut instinct knew better.

How many times does this happen when a vehicle is towed? I believe that was the only time I had heard such a thing. I knew deep down inside that, I was experiencing a news article I had read about. That night I was living the headlines.

Anxious to get off that roof, I felt I only had one choice left and that was my fire escape ladder. It was rolled up inside the loft that was at the front of my Winnie. What I called the loft was a camper shell I permanently mounted on the Winnebago replacing the roof in order to extend room for a bedroom.

I had to lean off the roof a bit, and reach over the camper shell window in order to reach the ladder. (Not an easy task for a one armed person.) I was not going to just sit and wait for the "supervisor".

I did managed to get the ladder out of the loft window. Iit unrolled perfectly, as I let it drop to the ground. I was wishing I had a few lessons in being a stunt double, as I tried to climb onto the ladder. I truly felt like I was in a Hollywood movie; instead of my own life at that moment. Who would ever believe our tax dollars supported such nonsense; until that moment, I never had imagined it.

The "driver" saw the ladder unroll, and demanded for me to remain up on the roof. Becoming a little annoyed; I threw him an obscene gesture, and began to climb onto the ladder. Being made of chain links, the ladder swayed back and forth, as I tried to climb down. The rungs were bolted onto the chains and that made it impossible to slide your hands down the ladder.

One week earlier, I had injured my left hand in a bicycle accident. I was trying to move some of our belongings that were still in the park to our Winnebago. I hung a jacket over the handle bars.

It slipped into the front tire and immediately stopped the bike. Me and the back half of the bike flipped over the front wheel. I shielded my face with my left arm which struck the curb causing my pinky finger to bend backwards at about a forty-five degree angle. It didn't break but instead it was so dislocated that the bone protruded out from the skin.

Even though I had only use of one arm, caution still never entered my mind. Fight or flight was in overdrive and my only thought was escape. I don't know how far down I got before I lost my footing and nearly fell off the ladder. I managed to catch myself by hugging the ladder with my arm that was in a caste.

The ladder swayed even more from my near slip, my heart skipped a beat as a bit of fear surged through me. I paused a moment and then proceeded to climb down. Again, I lost my footing.

This time my luck ran out and I failed to stop myself from slipping off the ladder.

Unfortunately, I wore rings on every finger back then, sometimes two or three. I did manage to catch myself, breaking my fall but the ring on my pinky finger was what kept me from hitting the ground.

Before I could blink an eye, I was hanging about three to four feet from the ground. (I saw my Great Grandfather loose his finger, and knew I had only seconds before I would lose mine.)

My freed arm happened to be in the caste. My only option I could think of was my feet. I quickly kicked my shoes off. (Luckily, I was not wearing socks.) I then curled and tucked my legs as close to my chest as possible; which allowed me to use my feet to push myself up a bit. That small push up, freed me and I fell to the ground. I landed on my back, knocking the wind out of me.

Hot, burning pain surged up my right arm and through my body. I felt like my hand was on fire. I could hear only pounding sound in my head as I tried to stand. My world spun and tinkle lights came into view as I began to try to walk, staggering and still trying to catch my breath as fear surged through me. I needed help but who and where.

I looked at my hand and much to my surprise, my finger was still there. At first glance, I could not see the two rings I had been wearing. As I quickly walked out of the parking lot, I looked at my finger again and saw a familiar sparkle of a stone. The two rings were imbedded into my finger!

Between the pulsating pain and the darkening colour, I knew I had to get those rings off. I tried to remove them but the swelling would not allow the rings to move. A hot, burning pain surged again up my arm as my finger turned from purple to black.

Half way out of the parking lot, I had caught my breath. I picked up the pace as I started to run towards the apartments across the street from the church. I was hoping to find help.

I only had to get to the end of the parking lot before I found a familiar face. I was relieved to see Matt, a person who was at the time, slowly becoming a great friend. Matt had no clue where I had the Winnebago parked. He was in the neighborhood and for some reason just happening to be carrying a working cell phone. (That was abnormal for the poor or homeless friends I had.) It was just a quince dance, and I was grateful for it. He took one look and quickly dialed 911. It was obvious that I needed help.

"Emergency is on their way" he reassured me as he continued listening to the operator for instructions. "Hold your arm up; it needs to be elevated."

Matt has such a kind soul. He is an easy person to like, and a loyal friend. I looked up at him, as I sat the curb. His five foot something, medium built frame, and dark complexion, glowed from sweat in the Arizona heat. I felt grateful to know such a person. His round face and chiseled features clearly told the anxiety that he was trying to with hold from me.

In the nearby distance, we heard the familiar sounds of fire and rescue. The sirens became louder as they came into view. After turning the corner onto the street we were on, the truck sped a bit and then drove past us.

"They just went past us," he said into the phone.

"I see them again," he spoke; as he stepped into the middle of the street and then waved his arms.

The emergency vehicle slowed, swerving past Matt, and going right by us again. I desperately wanted to laugh at that whole predicament by then, but I was in too much pain. The only sound I could utter was some inhuman like moaning.

"They did it again!" I heard Matt exclaim annoyingly into the phone. "Okay, okay…"

For the third time around the block a familiar bright red truck appeared, and finally slowed to a stop in front of us. Finally, help had arrived! Knowing that I was going to be all right; Matt disappeared just as quickly as he appeared early that afternoon.

I suffered from what is called a de-gloving. The skin, muscles, and tendons were cut down to the bone, and peeled back like a banana. I was very fortunate to have my finger still. A female fire fighter had never seen anyone be able to unhook him or herself in her ten-year career. None of them could even recall anyone who had not lost their finger from an accident like mine.

The fire fighters did not have any tools to cut my rings off. A crowd had been gathering by that point. My situation had become the Wednesday afternoon entertainment in the neighbourhood.

"Does anyone have a pair of wire cutters?" asked a fire fighter, to the crowd.

"I do," replied a stranger in the crowd; "I live only a few houses down."

"Please, go and get them," responded the fire fighter. "Hurry or she will lose her finger."

My finger was just about black in colour by then. The pain became even more unbearable. I was much relived to see the stranger return within minutes.

The first ring came off with ease, and I felt some of the pressure release. The second ring was no longer visible, and only I knew it was there. The intense pain made it impossible for me to talk, so I pushed the ring into visibility with my mobile fingers on my left hand. Finally, they could cut the imbedded band from my finger. The wound on my finger was cut even wider in the process, but the release of the pressure felt wonderful.

Sweat, and tears streamed down my face as I spoke my first tangible words to my rescuers.

"Thank you. Thank you so much," I said relived.

The pain had eased; but the wound was still bleeding terribly. When the ambulance team came onto the scene; I was urged to go with them, but I refused. My concern again was not for me but my Winnie. I strongly believed if I only explained to the officers, they would show some compassion towards me. I signed a waver so none of the rescuers could be held responsible for my well-being.

The police showed little or no empathy towards my situation or me. I was met instead with anger and disgust. They were cold and inhumane. No one on the scene would discuss anything with me. I was not allowed to explain or ask questions. I was treated as only a nuisance, other than that I was invisible. I never expected someone to just step up and hand me a golden ticket out of poverty. I did assume to be treated equally, one person to another.

All I wanted was a little respect as a person. Maybe a little acknowledgement that I was trying my best at what resources I had. At the very least, some advice on where I could receive help. Why was I treated so harshly? My conclusion is poverty.

My only crime was being poor. I had no record other than a traffic fine. I knew virtually no one so there were no visitors. I respected the fact I was on private property. I tried to show gratitude. I would try to explain my situation when needed.

I wanted everyone to know I did not choose to be a problem. I wanted as much as anyone to be out of the way, and not on his or her doorstep. I just had no idea of how to help myself. I lived day to day and did what I thought could help me. I felt like whatever I did was never enough or correct.

As I was placed in the back of the patrol car, an officer sneered a remark; that was directed at my concern about my finger.

"Why do we care about your finger you have nine other ones don't you?" he said mockingly.

The next hour or so became a bit of a blur. As I looked out the window, I watched the streets turn into avenues. The patrol car turned onto an on ramp and gathered speed as it sped down an Arizona highway. Soon Phoenix Streets appeared again. I felt the driver turn onto another on ramp and pause for oncoming traffic. Once again, I was being driven around the west side of phoenix.

I began to wonder if we were headed to any destination at all, as I tried hard not to listen to the officers' bereavement. Suffering from shock I feel helped me to block the mental bashing. I did not know if I should feel scared, worried or both; at the time.

"Society would be better off without scum like you," sneered an officer from the front seat. "I bet no one would miss you."

Again, I tried hard not to listen, but a few degrading words slipped through my invisible wall. It was difficult to hold back tears, but I chose to show no emotion. I was not going to give them any more power or satisfaction from my sufferings.

Instead, I hid inside myself, slipping into the dark corners of my mind and shielding myself emotionally as much as I could.

I could sense they wanted me to respond with anger and hate. I knew the officers wanted me to lash out, to fight back or in the very least cry from being belittled. I was routine abuse for them. I felt that the officers looked at me as less than human. I was an object used to release daily frustrations. Their actions indicated to me that I was not their first victim and unfortunately probably not their last.

Eventually, the gauze wrap became soaked with blood. Concerned, I asked, "Are we almost to the jail? I am bleeding quite a bit; the wrap is soaked."

I was given no reply. Silence filled the car for the first time since I had been in it. The hum from the engine was the only sound that could be heard. The tires rumbling on the road became eerie as it made sounds of slowing speed.

I looked around trying to see if I would know where we were, but nothing seemed familiar. The car drove down an on ramp and slowed even more. It was clear to me that the squad car was slowing to a stop.

The officers made eye contact with each other, but neither of them said anything. They had obviously done this countless time's before. As the vehicle edged towards the shoulder, I could hear only the sound of my heart.

Only miles of highway and endless desert landscape could be seen out of the window. Overwhelming panic surged through me. I was literally trapped.

My only way out was controlled by the police officers. I tried not to replay the old Hollywood movie scripts that entered my thoughts.

Instead, I told myself to just keep breathing I as I tried not to show how frightened I really was. The officer pulled off the road and put the car into park. I heard the sound of the door latch release as the driver stepped out of the vehicle. Moments later he opened my door and ordered me to get out.

My immediate thought was; out of the car but why? I was shaking so much that I could almost hear my bones rattle. I never really knew how fear felt until that day. I had been afraid many times in my life, but until that day, I realized I had never felt it.

My legs were shaking so much that I had wondered if they would collapse beneath me as I stepped out of the vehicle. My legs wobbled as I stood face to face with the officer. Terrified, I fought the urge to run when I was outside the car. Even though fleeing was my first instinct, I knew it would not help my situation.

I was at their mercy. Not only was I was physically helpless; I was incapable of any legal aid as well. Who could save me from the police? Who would believe my story if they could help me? My sense of security no longer existed at that moment. That day I became very afraid of everything and everyone around me.

The officer's hand came towards me; I closed my eyes not wanting to imagine what could possibly happen next. I jumped as I heard the car door slam shut. I stared at the officer in disbelief as he took a couple steps away from me and started to return to the driver's seat.

Before he shut his door, the officer looked back at me and said, "Don't walk on the highway, or you will be arrested."With that said he shut his door and drove off leaving me to digest what I had just been through.

I collapsed sobbing with relief and fear. The stress of the situation and loosing so much blood made me feel very cold, tired, and weak.

I knew I had to get back to where the officers picked me up, but I had no clue where I was. I wondered if I was still in Phoenix.

As I walked up the on ramp and onto a sidewalk, I saw a gentleman walking towards me. "Am I still in Phoenix?" I asked.

He didn't have to respond. By the expression upon his face, I knew that I was indeed still in Phoenix. "Never mind"' I replied realizing immediately that my question was probably the strangest thing he had ever heard.

I had on untied, white tennis shoes. Spots of blood were visible evidence that told their own story of its owner's ordeal. Looking down at my feet; I wished for one of two things, and they were: first, the ability to use of at least one hand and second, to know in which direction I had to go.

Little did I know at the time, I was about to walk ten miles. Several years later; I would learn, that the officers had dropped me off about ten miles away from where I had parked the Winnebago, and I was about eight miles away from a hospital. Years later I would also discover, what I had embarked on, is known as a death march. The homeless in Phoenix, Arizona are the ones who have come to call it that.

At that moment in time; I knew nothing about homeless death marches or how far I was about to walk. I only knew that I needed to find my area of Phoenix, so I looked around hoping for a clue in which direction to go. Nothing seemed familiar. I felt like a foreigner in a city I called home for years. I regretted always allowing Joe to find our way through the city. I felt so stupid for being so naive and trusting. All the regret I held could not help me so I started walking hoping I was heading in the right direction. I could have tossed a coin and got the same amount of luck.

I knew I had to find Thirty-Second Street. I noticed that the street I was on was on forty something. I watched the street signs and quickly realized they were going up instead of down; unfortunately I was walking in the wrong direction.

I was tired, exhausted and weak by the time I figured out I was walking totally in the wrong direction. I just wanted to wake up and have that complete day be nothing but a nightmare.

After I started to walk in the correct direction, I finally saw a familiar landmark. As I pushed my way through groups of people, I saw a familiar sign that read: Park and Swap.

That location was a familiar spot for me since I was a vender there quite often. It was Wednesday night and crowds of people were coming to the Swap mart in hopes of a good deal.

I walked by not just one or two people, but hundreds of people. Not one person took enough time or concern to see if they could help. My appearance was obvious that I was in need of help, but the only response I received was stares. I never asked for help, but I could not imagine walking by someone looking as I did and not asking him or her if I could assist in some way.

What is our world coming to?? Has our society really become that self- involved? Are we as a nation so petty that offering a hand has become too much to ask?

I pushed on determined to make it back to the Winnebago. I was not sure if it still was in that church lot; I just knew I must try to get back there. My feet and legs felt so heavy as my untied shoes became more cumbersome with every step. I tried not to pay attention to the speeding traffic, as I walked down one of the busiest streets in Phoenix during rush hour.

I noticed the famous, beautiful, pink, Phoenician sunset; as the sun slowly began to set. The more the sun sat; the colder I felt. Oddly, I felt no pain from my severed finger. The blood soaked wrap was beginning to make my hand unbearably cold, so I tried to hold my arm close to me.

After a couple of miles, my untied shoes became impossible to wear. I tried to keep them on my feet but the more I walked the looser they became. As I crossed 32nd St. and McDowell, (a busy intersection in Phoenix); I walked out of both shoes. I tried to gather up my shoes, as the light turned green. Arrogant drivers with absolutely holding no concern for anyone but himself or herself honked. I guess the noise is supposed to make someone like myself, move quicker.

By that time of the day, I was more than a little annoyed by how I was being treated that day. Frustration, anger, and hurt emotions took over as I lashed out at one of the inconsiderate drivers. I hit the hood of a big, older, bronze colored and gas guzzler of a car with my left arm (that was the in a cast), as I yelled "I'm f**king walking here."

I only remember saying that sentence to the traffic; after that, what I said is a blur. I do remember that not one car went through that light. No one moved nor did they honk again. I guess no one wanted to push an injured psycho any farther. I would like to think maybe I made someone think about the situation, but I doubt that.

The next thing I recall is the light turning red again. I realized at that time I was acting like a mad woman and quickly walked down the road. I was finally in a familiar area of Phoenix. I knew I was only few blocks away from my friend's house. I hoped to find some help there or in the least warm up a bit.

The sun had set and the streetlights were coming on by the time I turned the corner of my friend's block. I could see Todd's tall, lanky figure outside as I walked closer to his place.

He helped me put on an extra sweater he had in his closet. Then he wrapped more gauze around my right hand and arm.

I could see the concern in his big brown eyes as he urged me to go to the hospital. His long face seemed even longer from despair as I agreed but only after I found out what had happened to my home. I knew he understood how I felt and my rationalization towards my situation.

The Winnebago, for me, was much more than a vehicle; it was my house. Just like most people who are not homeless, everything I owned and treasured was inside my residence. Only society considered me homeless when I owned the Winnie. As for myself, I was not homeless but my home was.

It was about a mile and a half walk from my friend's house to the church where I had parked. The anxiety I felt grew more overwhelming as I got closer to the church. "Please be there," I whispered to myself.

As I turned the corner of the parking lot, I was so relieved to see the Winnie still located in the spot that I had left it. It was untouched and unharmed! I had won the battle that day. I was a little banged up and injured but none the least I had won!

Chapter Three

SOCIETY

The morning after being hung up on the ladder, I realized how bad I was injured. I had my friend Rick, help me cut the gauze bandage off. His stocky stature seemed shorter as he leaned forward holding onto to stomach trying not to be sick. His round face and brown eyes showed concern.

"Wrap it up, Storm. That is so gross, he said pleadingly.

My finger was a nauseating sight as it fell effortlessly to the outside of my hand. As it hung limply, we could both see the bone since the skin was rolled back from the wound. What looked like red and blue string protruded out of the cut; was in reality muscle and tendons. The rest of my finger was a dark purple to black color. I had no feeling in that finger nor could I move it. My finger felt cold to the touch. I felt as though I did lose my finger.

After my hand was rewrapped, I sat down inside my Winnie. I sat in the middle of the floor with my legs crossed and placed my wrapped arms on top of my lap. I then looked down at them and cried until I had no tears left.

As tears rolled down my cheeks and unto the floor, I wondered what next. How was I going to survive? What did my future hold? Would I ever be able to be an artist again?

Daily life was hard enough. Without the ability to use either hand was a disadvantage I knew would be hard to recover from. I feared the worse, but hoped for the best.

I felt as though karma had betrayed me. What did I do that was so wrong? The one thing I thought could never be taken I had just lost. My hands were like taking legs from a runner, or hearing from a musician.

I yearned for normalcy at that moment. I wanted so very much to be able to crawl into bed, take something for the pain and heal like anyone else in society would have done. Even though I was considered unemployed I had no time to sit.

Time wasn't something I had, nor did it hold any meaning to me. When I became transitionally homeless the hands on the clock moved forward, but I remained still. I became an outsider looking in upon society. The world was moving on without me in it. I watched helplessly each day go by and saw how the season's change. If I wanted to move forward with my life I knew I could not stand still. Every minute that passed added up to another day. Days could add up to months and then years of remaining worthless. I was not worthless. I knew one day, time and myself; would be in sync again, but only if I did not stop trying.

As much as I wanted to I didn't give up. I quickly adapted to not being able to use both arms. I even had figured out a way to keep up the dumpster findings!! I used my legs to get in and out of dumpsters. To get in I would put one leg over the ledge of the dumpster and pretty much roll in. Getting in was easy. Climbing back out has always been the difficult part of dumpster diving.

Even with the use of both arms I always found it complicated to climb out. Since the use of my arms was limited I put both legs over the dumpster's ledge while leaning back on the trash.

70

I then would do a sit up to get out. It wasn't easy but in the least I received a wonderful looking abs from my nightly work out.

My life unraveled quickly after losing the use of both arms. Limited use of both hands and arms is difficult enough for someone that is not homeless. Being homeless with limitations leaves a person vulnerable to a whole new world of misery.

I became a target for every type of abuse. Thieves like to buddy up to a vulnerable person that is still dangling on the edge of becoming homeless. During those months of disability I met some of the strangest people.

With a little help from what I thought to be new found friends. I managed to get the Winnebago up and running again. For the first time in years the Winnebago finally had working breaks!

After working on the Winnebago for about one in one week I was finally able to drive it out of the church parking lot. Being able to drive the Winnie; was a short lived victory. It felt like no matter where I went or what I did; it was never enough to for the Phoenix police. The officers would always find some reason to knock on my Winnebago. None of the officers offered anything but harassment towards my situation. By then most of the Phoenix police officers in that area knew me. I would try to explain as politely as possible to the few offices that I did not know that I didn't know Phoenix and would accept any advice or help. If any of the officers believed my situation they chose not to offer advice or help.

February 14th 2003; I lost the Winnebago war. It became a day I will never forget and one I relive every year. That day the battle started with a knock at my door. It was around 11:30 AM. A shivering tingle swept over my spine; I knew nothing good would come from that knock.

"This can't be good." I mumbled to myself as I looked at my watch.

I knew that day would become one of those long days on the battlefield. I had come to the conclusion by then; earlier someone would knock the longer the more grueling than day would be.

"Put on your battle gear", I said to Richard, who happened to be visiting at the time.

He just shook his head as he kind of chuckled towards my odd sense of humor. He watched as I reluctantly climbed onto the roof down the ladder.

I was not at all surprised to see the police knocking on my door. Game on; I thought to myself. At the same time I wondered who would win that day.

"Good morning officers," I said politely; keeping my thoughts to the situation to myself.

I had forgotten to remove a tow sticker that the police had placed on the Winnebago while parked at a different location. I pointed out that the locations were different. They assumed as trying to be brazen towards them because I had moved only 4 to 5 blocks.

"I ran out of gas," I said pleadingly. "I was planning on getting some gas this afternoon after I sold my gift baskets."

"You have an excuse for everything; don't you?" said a female officer impatiently.

After a small battle of wits, the officers on scene agreed finally to have the Winnebago towed to my friend's trailer. The police officers promised if I could have $100 in hand; that the Winnebago would not be impounded. I had no choice but to agree with them. At the time I still had a false sense of security in our justice system.

I went back inside the Winnebago and grabbed a backpack full of items I knew I could sell easily. I knew someone would help me make up the difference if I could not make the money myself.

"If you don't have the one hundred dollars the tow truck driver won't drop the Winnebago," yelled an officer to me as I walked off.

Richard didn't think they would actually tow it anywhere; since the Winnebago had been threatened to be towed many times before. He wanted to stay inside and avoid the drama.

I tried to change his mind but in the end I left him behind. I walked the two miles to my friend's house lost in my thoughts.

By then I was little more aware of how some of the Phoenix police held an attitude of disdain arrogance; towards the homeless. Again I was powerless towards their disparagement. I do not want to trust them but had no choice to do as they asked. I just hoped for once the police were showing compassion and not being cruel.

I realized later that afternoon that I was wrong again. I was sitting on Todd's steps when I saw Richard walking towards me. I had been sitting on the step with $100's in hand for a few hours by then.

"What is going on?" I asked in desperation.

"I'm sorry, Storm, they took it," he replied.

I felt as though I was suffocating. The money slipped out of my hand as a clasped to my knees. I wanted to scream but no sound could I make.

Todd came outside of his trailer to comfort me. Without a second thought, he said "Don't worry about not having a place. My place is your place."

I took a moment before I said, "Thank you."

I tried to stay positive. I thought to myself; I know where to go but up. Little did I foresee; that there was so much more to lose.

Looking back, I know now; you lose the unspoken things of life that no one realizes they own.

Losing the Winnebago did not end the war for me. That day I was left with only the clothes on my back. Inside the Winnebago laid all the information of addresses and phone numbers to everyone I ever knew. I was suddenly trapped in phoenix. The only option I had left was to stay and hope something would happen in my favor.

I only shared Todd's place for a short time. Even though he meant well, Todd had problems of his own. In less than a month, he had a warrant out for his arrest, and was taken into custody.

I fell into a crowd that camped behind a house. The campsite was an endless place of drama.

In my opinion, the homeless develop a society of its own. Like the general society, the homeless society, is more complex and informal. I feel the homeless society seems more primitive than the general one.

What I observed is the homeless society goes back to the caveman days. A day when hunters and gatherers ruled; and each clan had their own unwritten law. When I was on the streets, the homeless lived and worked similar to those caveman ancestors.

The superstitious belief is the homeless do not work. The truth is I learned is people who are homeless work at everyday living. There are not enough hours in a day to find food, shelter, and resources. Though; some people do live independently on the streets. Being homeless myself, I found it nearly impossible to do so. I like so many others, discovered early on living in the streets of Phoenix; that connecting with a street family was more beneficial.

My family clan was similar to other street families. Everyone in my group had their own unspoken rules to help the group function day to day. Someone unspoken led and directed. The leaders of groups are easy to recognize. Those people are the first to step up and protect others in the group and almost always speak for others. They are also people who give orders to those in the group, and help keep chaos to a minimal. Roles I found in a street family can change from day to day but more often than not they don't.

There are some of those stereotyped individuals who are homeless that everyone is familiar with. Those people are what general society thinks of all homeless to be; and that is worthless mooch who just doesn't want to work. What the general society doesn't realize is the homeless society loath those individuals just as much. For one reason it is because of those individuals that the stereotypes exist. Another reason is not only do they use general society to survive the use the homeless as well.[7]

---

7 On the next few pages I added more stories of brutality

Violence Against the Homeless

It was August 1999 in the Lealman area of Pinellas County,Florida, near St. Petersburg, and Don Regnier was at u bus stop on the 4700 block of 28th St. North, near what is now Lealman Intermediate School. He apparently waved his arms at a passing car complaining about a loud stereo. The car stopped and two men got out. They punched and kicked him to death. Don Regnier, age 51, was homeless.

People who knew him in the area liked him and said he never bothered anyone and was always friendly.Tony Rosa, 19, recieved a life term for killing Mr. Regnier. At sentencing, Judge Federico stated "It's sad that Mr. Regnier paid the price for the criminal justice systems failure". Rosa had a history of criminal violations, and was serving house arrest at the time of the killing instead of a 60 month
prison term.

It's not unusual for homeless people to be beaten, often severely, and robbed of the little they have, even their shoes. Such assaults rarely get any mention in the media unless there is a fatality. It's not worthwhile "news". A 2006 study commissioned by the Association of Gospel Rescue Missions indicated that nearly 1 in 5 homeless people had been attacked during the past year.

I have experienced being homeless and learned the hard way about being careful on the street. When I had to camp, I did so out of view so I couldn't be easily found at night. While some fear the dark, it's protection for those avoiding being the victim of assault and rob

Even so I have been attacked more than a couple times. Many others I know have been beaten, sometimes severely. One friend of mine was attacked at night, while he was in his sleeping bag, by a couple guys with pipes. He was able to get up and run for help to some friends in a nearby camp.

They helped him get to the nearby university hospital. Both university police and local police came down on the area but couldn't find the perpetrators. He ended up with hundreds of stitches on his face, but if he hadn't been able to get away he would probably have been killed.

Attacks like these usually have nothing to do with robbery. More often it's by people that just think it's "entertainment" to beat up homeless people. Apparently they don't have the mental capacity to comprehend morality.

The National Coalition for the Homeless has been collecting information on violence against the homeless. In their listing of data from 1999 to 2002 Florida ranks eighth in the nation as most dangerous for the homeless while California ranks first. The worst city in the US was Denver, Colorado, with 9 deaths during that period. Overall, 131 homeless people were murdered during this period (by available statistics). These are based on what little is reported to police. Much more of the violence goes unreported. No one really knows how many homeless are killed. It seldom gets in the news in this area about homeless being beaten, even with police responding, since it's so common.

The results of a study released by the National Coalition for the Homeless (2-20-2007) rated the state of Florida as the most violent toward the homeless, with almost three times as many assaults as the second most violent state, Arizona.

2/2008:

According to the National Coalition for the Homeless and the National Law Center on Homelessness and Poverty most of the 142 unprovoked attacks on homeless people in 2007 were in Florida. Nationwide attacks in 2007 were 65% higher than in 2005.

One time an officer came to my camp and told me that I shouldn't be camping there. He pointed out that it's wasn't private property and I was doing nothing illegal, but said it was too dangerous and I should get into a shelter. I agreed that it was dangerous, but pointed out that it's nearly impossible to get into a shelter, even with special needs.

There weren't enough shelter beds for even 10% of the homeless. The city of St. Petersburg was considering making it illegal for homeless people to camp together in public areas, even though they do it for safety. It was said that they will be offered a ride to a shelter, though there are not enough beds available for more than a few of these people, and just for a few days.

The number of homeless sleeping on the streets in St. Petersburg has risen dramatically over the last few years. One Sunday morning I was walking to church downtown and saw several people in blankets on the steps of City Hall, and many in the downtown park. Some cities are actually working on constructive programs to help people get off the street, and making real progress, instead of just jailing people for being homeless.

Much of the violence has been by gangs of teenagers, out to stalk and beat homeless people with pipes, bricks, or baseball bats. Some try to legitimize it by calling it "bum hunting", as if it were a sport. To some young people, lacking any sense of moral values, it's just something to do for entertainment. Beating homeless people happens every day, and is increasing. Statistics indicate that 33% of hate crimes are committed by those under age 18. Beating and killing homeless isn't currently considered a hate crime, but then what is it?

In May 2005, Michael Eugene Roberts, a 53 year old homeless man, was killed in Holly Hill, near Daytona FL. It was a brutal and totally deliberate murder. There was no apparent motive of robbery or revenge. Two 18 year olds and three under 18 have been arrested on murder charges. A couple of the teens stated that they attacked the man "for fun" and "to have something to do".

4/24/06:

Four teens were sentenced to between 22 and 35 years in Florida state prison in the death of Michael Roberts. All pleaded guilty to

2nddegree murder and conspiracy to commit murder.Would they have gotten off this easily if the person they killed wasn't homeless? If the victim was well known and respected they would all probably be serving life, if not receiving the death penalty. If they survive prison (and many don't) they may be homeless on the street for the rest of their lives, just like their victim. Warren Messner, who was 15 then, is now 18 and serving a 22 year prison term for his part in the attack. He doesn't think it's so much fun today.

In January 17, 2007, two homeless men, Jeffery Schultz, 43, and David Heath, 53, were shot and killed in a quiet neighborhood of St. Petersburg, FL, late at night. It appeared that robbery was involved, though neither of the men had anything of value to steal.

2/8/07:

Dorion Deshawn Dillard, 20, and Cordaro Antwan Hardin, 18, were arrested on charges of first degree murder in the deaths of the two homeless men. Two others have been identified in connection with the murders but have not yet been arrested.

The incidents described here are only a few of those that received media attention, and the figures in surveys only include those that were reported. The real numbers are far higher, perhaps several times these figures. No reporters ever visited me in the hospital. Articles on assaults on the homeless don't sell newspapers unless the incident is particularly gruesome, and selling advertising space is what newspapers are all about. Meanwhile assaults and killing of the homeless go on every day across our great nation, and keep increasing.

In the state of Florida there is a death penalty for first degree murder. If someone kills a child, a mother, or someone respected by the community, they will probably get the death penalty in Florida. Kill a homeless person, even if premeditated and violent, and you may get 20 years, if not far less

.I don't doubt that many of the attackers have mental problems. Some just have no value for the lives of others, and *eventually are* removed from *contact with civilization. Some die in prison at the hands of their own kind. How many innocent people have to die first?*

Often homeless people are victims of other homeless who will steal anything, and destroy what they can't steal. These are usually those who never had real parents or grew up in households with no moral guidance whatsoever. There are many parents that teach their children to be criminals, and as a result they know nothing else. Many spend most of their lives in-and-out of county jails or state prison, and many die there without ever comprehending what it's like to live a normal life. Since they never learned anything about earning a living they just waste away doing petty crimes. There are families where this continues from generation to generation.

At Esplanade Park in Ft. Lauderdale, Florida, in September of 2006, a homeless man, William Teeters was punched, kicked, and slashed by a group of teenagers. His friend, Norris Gaynor, had been beaten to death in the same park in January of that same year.

In March 2008 two of the teens that attacked Teeters, Michael Livingston, 16, and Patrick Keels, 17, were sentenced in court for attempted murder in the unprovoked attack.

They could have received maximum sentences of 90 years and 40 years respectively, however when Teeters addressed the court he asked for mercy toward them saying "I want them to have the second chance I wish I had got," and "I went to an adult prison when I was underage and it only made me harder."

As a result the two were sentenced to two years in prison plus four years probation.

Another teen, Bobby Callins, 18, had also been sentenced to two years in the attack, and Romel Jean-Louis, 17, is to be sentenced, probably for juvenile detention. The teens who killed Gaynor are to go on trial in the summer of 2008. (Information from the Miami Herald, 3/15/2008, miamiherald.com)

Another kind of assault goes on quietly every month. This is where homeless people who get disability or social security payments are robbed of whatever they have, typically by drug addicts. When government payments go out at the beginning of the month, suddenly people appear out of nowhere and go after the homeless people who get payments but are either physically or mentally not capable of defending themselves. "Hey buddy, could you help me out with some money?" While the homeless person may get $600 or more, much of it is gone in a day, and the a rarely even gets reported. It happens thousands of times every month all across the country.[8]

8 The next few pages contain an article about the homeless population booming.

Homeless in America

Posted: 12.11.02

Federal and local agencies are struggling to help a growing number of families forced out of their homes by an unsteady economy and quickly rising housing prices. Cities around the country are reporting record numbers of homeless people entering shelters or sleeping on the streets. As a faltering U.S. economy, skyrocketing housing prices and reduced government services force people from their homes, agencies are scrambling to find ways to provide shelter and assistance to a growing and changing homeless population.

The National Law Center on Homelessness and Poverty estimates some 3 million men, women and children will be homeless for at least some part of 2002.

"I suspect it is going to be a record increase this year, as it was last year," Maria Foscarinis, executive director of the organization said in a Washington Post interview. "And it really does have to do with the economy, mainly loss of jobs and loss of wage-earning power."

An Unexpected Rise

Ater a Los Angeles earth-
quake, this young boy and
his family became homeless.

The face of homelessness has drastically changed throughout the years. In the 1980s, thousands of individuals from the nation's public psychiatric hospitals were discharged, leaving many of the country's mentally ill without homes. This gave rise to a popular misconception, however, that led many to think all homeless people were mentally ill or suffered from drug or alcohol abuse problems. Oftentimes, homeless people were portrayed as lazy and unclean.

But today, more working and middle class families face the prospect of living on the streets.

The Department Housing and Urban Development (HUD),

81

the federal agency in charge of housing issues, released the most complete report on homelessness in the U.S. The report, "The Forgotten Americans - Homelessness: Programs and the People They Serve," revealed that some 11 million Americans have "worst case" housing needs, putting them at a high risk of homelessness. Many are either spending over half of their paycheck on housing -- often doubled up with others in overcrowded conditions -- or live in houses that are falling apart.

Attempts to Diminish the Problem

Local and national agencies are seeking more creative means to combat homelessness, although not all are popular. In New York, where a record number of people are homeless, a judge blocked Mayor Michael Bloomberg's request to use an abandoned Bronx jail as housing.

Homeless men in a Brooklyn soup kitchen eat a meal prepared by volunteers.

More recently, Bloomberg proposed using retired cruise ships docked at city piers as shelters, an idea that troubled advocates for the homeless.

"It's disturbing," Patrick Markee of the Coalition for the Homeless told the New York Times. "Putting outcast people offshore -- there's something punitive about it."

"The assumption was that intervention was more important than prevention. Until now, government was misdiagnosing the condition and prescribing inadequate medicine." A more likely solution is placing more emphasis on permanent housing. Under HUD Secretary Mel Martinez, the agency adopted a "Housing First" policy and created a federal grant initiative called the SRO, or Single Room Occupancy, program. The program gives money to public agencies to fix single room housing units in an attempt to provide a more permanent alternative to traditional shelters. Martinez says he would like to see the end of chronic homelessness

within the next ten years.

One of the strongest federal attempts to end homelessness is to strengthen the already existing Stewart B. McKinney Homeless Assistance Act, the only major federal law concerning homelessness. That act provides money for emergency shelters, health care and job training, as well as education for homeless children.

This year, Sen. Jack Reed of Rhode Island introduced a new bill, the Community Partnership to End Homelessness Act of 2002, which would create a more united plan of providing increased funding at the community level.

"We want to provide adequate resources, emphasize the continuity of care, and hopefully not institutionalize homelessness in America, but end it," Reed said.

HUD Secretary Mel Martinez wants homelessness ended within the next ten years.

Politicians "For many years, Washington focused on and social workers looking for ways to end homelessness know that there are no easy answers, especially when many Americans notice the problem only when the weather turns cold and the situation more desperate. "No one wants to see homeless people suffering in the cold, but effective solutions are not easy," Arnold Cohen, president of Partnership for the Homeless, said. –

By Raven Tyler, News Hour Extra (Tyler, 2009)

A homeless man sleeps on a grate to try and keep warm during the winter months.

SURVIVAL

After pulling into Pac'n Stor; I put the car into park and pulled the keys out of the ignition. Today, a key still holds a lot of in depth meaning for me. I once took for granted the denotation a key represents. A person who has a key has a home, a car, and a place to go. They belong somewhere.

The
year of 2007 made records for the coldest days in about seventeen
years. At night, the temperatures fell below freezing; while the
general population turned on their heaters; the homeless clung to
each other and to their memories for warmth.

Almost two years had passed before I finally had enough nerve to open the vault of my past. That vault was a storage unit number eighty-seven on the shadier side of phoenix.

It was all I could afford at that time in my life. It took every penny I had and then some to have some place to call my own. At the time I was ecstatic to be able to legally claim someplace as my own.

That storage was my space, and no one could rule over how I used it. No one could take what little I gained and worked for. I finally held a key of hope to a better future. I knew my nightmare was far from over but I felt some glimmer of hope at the time.

Today the shiny dollar store lock was so rusted that it barely opened. As I opened the row laden door, spider webs inches deep greeted me. Beyond the web curtain laid a homeless person's treasure. Today I don't see much more than junk.

Stale air comes out of the storage unit as I pulled the door open. The 5 by 7 storage held another world. A time and place far different than the one I was living now yet a part of me still lingered in that time capsule amongst the objects.

I again felt every tear I shed while fighting to keep what I had inside that storage unit. Flicker of images from the past flashed through my mind. A haunting shiver sent tingles through me, as I again relived the turmoil of my past.

At that moment, I sensed her, my past self. A person who became so defeated and broken stared back at me. She was a shadow of me but at that moment, I barely knew her. She was so entrapped by fatal mistakes and desperately wanting to be free from the shackles that burdened her. That person was someone who became so lost that even she thought it would be a miracle to find her. A miracle she thought would never happen.

Somehow, that miracle did happen, but how or when I was not very sure. A sense of relief filled my heart as I came to the understanding that I had found the freedom from being helpless. I knew at that moment I was on my way to stability.

My greatest fear of reliving a homeless life subsided a bit and I was overcome by a feeling of gratitude from the insight knowing that not everyone; will make it through the core. I was fortunate; I had a place to call home. I had the luxury of feeling safe and secure. My life was no longer in jepordy.

Every day, homeless people parish in the United States. Living on the streets of America isn't sanitary or safe. When you lose a door to lock at night; your safe haven no longer exists. Sleeping; becomes a dangerous luxury.

Homeless Veterans Burial Program Spreads *<u>Thursday, May 22, 2003</u>, 8:23 AM By **<u>Bob Priddy</u>**; A program begun in St. Louis four years ago to provide proper burials to homeless veterans has spread to more than ten cities and has provided military burials to about 150 people. More than 30 of those burials have been in the St. Louis region. The Homeless Veterans Burial Program steps in when family members cannot afford to pay for the burial. The funeral industry picks up some of the costs, including that of a casket. The federal Veterans Affairs Department estimates there are more than five-thousand homeless veterans in Missouri.* (Priddy, 2003)

The Los Angeles County Coroner's Office handled 205 indigent deaths from July to December 2007, and 404 from Jan. 1 to June 30, 2009, a 97 percent increase. (Lacey Peterson, 2009)

From the Dean of Sydney, Phillip Jensen; *This week in our Square just outside St Andrew's House a man was killed. He was twenty-three years old*

His violent end stands in stark contrast to the message of life that we seek to preach in this place. His brutal death is poignantly tragic as we approach the celebrations of the birth of our Lord and Savior.

Most of the homeless around us are addicted to some substance, usually alcohol. But that is often one of the symptoms of the problem rather than the cause. They usually come from distressing circumstances of family breakdown. They have often endured terrible psychiatric episodes. They have made unwise life skill choices that have given them very few resources to deal with their long-term problems.

9The following article contains a few stories of those who died in the core. Like I have said and will say again, '...not everybody can or will make it through the core.'

The spiral downwards through addiction into destitute hopelessness is a sad and tragic journey. There is little point telling them to "pull up their socks", "get out of bed", "get a job". They have no socks, they have no bed, and they do not have the emotional, physical or social energy to re-enter the workforce. By the time they reach the streets the system of our society has beaten them.

But it does bring home to us the power of evil in our city and the plight of so many vulnerable people, especially the homeless. (Jensen, 2006)

Homeless Memorial Day

Each year since 1990, on or near the first day of winter and the longest night of the year, National Coalition for the Homeless (NCH) has sponsored National Homeless Persons' Memorial Day to bring attention to the tragedy of homelessness and to remember our homeless friends who have paid the ultimate price for our nation's failure to end homelessness. This year, the National Health Care for the Homeless Council (NHCHC) has joined us in co-sponsoring this event.

In an effort to maximize the impact of the day, NCH and the NHCHC have encouraged local and statewide organizations to hold memorials of their own. Last year, over 100 cities across the nation, from Detroit to Seattle to Washington, DC, sponsored events to honor those who had died and to recommit to the task of ending homelessness.

This Year, once again, NCH is encouraging groups to plan a special event on or around December 21, 2009. Some groups may decide to hold their event a day or so before the date.

(Homeless, 2008)

Nationwide List of Homeless Persons Who Died in 2008

Below is a list of individuals who were honored at services and vigils around the country in 2008. The numbers attached to each location represent only those who were currently homeless and who died in 2008, but names of others—including formerly homeless individuals or advocates for the homeless—who were also remembered at the memorials were included if provided by the local community. Some communities did not release the names of the people honored for privacy reasons.

ALABAMA

MOBILE (13)
Isadore Beck
Willie Bryant
Russell Chestnut
Nathaniel Crosby
Joseph Michael Dailey
Jacqueline Davis
Michael Hawkins
Jennifer Horn
Robert Johnson
Garcia Parker
Robert Powe
Lugene Taylor
Vanya Woods

ARIZONA

TUCSON (128)
Burials at the Pima County Cemetery, November 2007-October 2008
Today we remember:
45 people without name or family
30 people with names and family
53 people with names only, no family

ARKANSAS
LITTLE ROCK (15)

CALIFORNIA

LOS ANGELES – STUDIO CITY (393)
Edward Adams, Jr.
Jorge Adane
David Aguirre
Antonio Alanis
Alhakim

Sandra Aliano
"Twin A" Allen
"Twin B" Allen
Gonzalo Alonso
Jayme Amaresco
Jorge Amezcua
Carl C Anderozzi
Abel Andrade
Daniel Araujo
Gilbert Arciniega
Hugo Arguemedo
Armando
John Aschmann
Jason Ashley
Juan Ayala
Larry Bables
Edison Bahe
Allen Banks
Bernadine Barringer
Samuel Beckner
Clifford Bedford
John Belles
Cesar Benidicto
Robert Bennett II
Edward Berch
Gary Bergstrom
Manuel Berrios
Ruth Berry
John Bittle
Lauren Black
Robert Blake
Anita Bonthius
Janice Booker
Eric Borsting
Ronald Bowen
Christopher Bowman
James Bowman
Ray Boyd
Richard Bradshaw

Delbert Thompson
Kauri Tryme, 39
Gabriel Torres-Reyes, 51
Bryce Turk, 33
Doug Vaughn, 47
Glen Vavarek
Diana Vigil, 50
Phillip Vigil, 55
Koji Wada, 63
Charles Walls, 30
Shirley Welch, 56
Barry Alan Wheeler, 52
Stephen Wheeler, 55
Stephen White, 38
William Whitelance
David Williams, 38
Ralph Wolcott
Dawn Wynkoop, 55
David Young, 52
Keith Young, 51
Felix Zamora, 25

PUEBLO (15)
Curtis Chavez, 37
Ted Garcia, 61
Linda Henson, 59
Daryl Holt, 48
Frances Jagger, 66
Linda Knoll, 47
April Passero, 54
Joseph Ponce, 53
Thomas Reynolds, 40
Randy Riggs, 42
Robin Sanchez, 43
Nettie Solano, 63
Jeffrey Trujillo, 42
Joseph Vigil, 48
Jean Yarbrough, 86

CONNECTICUT
BRIDGEPORT (16)

HARTFORD (7)
Estracio F.
Jeff L.
Leroy L.

Inocencio Q.
Kirk T.
Kenny W.
Timothy W.

MIDDLETOWN (3)
Oliver
Robert
Thomas

NEW BRITAIN (5)
Edwin
Eve
Jane
Julie
Marvin

NEW LONDON (7)
Larry Ager
Peter Dill
Andrew Fox
Robert Jasperson
Lester Osbourne
Richard Perry
William Williams

NORWICH (1)
Antonio Rivera
All those who died homeless in 2008
unknown

DISTRICT OF COLUMBIA
WASHINGTON (52)
Luis Admore
Darnell Alston
Orin Andres (former Street
                    Sense vendor)
Eric Barber
Larry Barnes
James Lee Carter
Charles Cole
Ms. Costello
Karen Ann Crawford
Michael Defonzo
Margarita Figueroa
Charles Ford

Miles Frazier
Patrice Gbengoue
Howard Hall
Eugene Hampton
Glen Harding
Malcolm Hatchett
Freddie Hilton
Robert Holly
Eddie Hopkins
Charles Jackson
Ms. Kenley
Kevin Madison
Antonia Parker
Larry Perkins
Stephen Prue
James Raines
Curtis Reed
Helen Richardson
Eric Robinson
Gregory Shea
Kenneth Lee Simmons
Walter Smith
Wilbur Smith
Lavona Turner
Isaac Umoh
George Ward
Harold J. Washington
Lawrence Watson
Robert Wylie
Jane Doe
John Doe

ALEXANDRIA, VA (9)
Sedric Barnes
Lawrence Bates
David Castle
Alfreida Cordero
Frank Hubert
Lincoln Nguyen
James Rector
Jackie Rivers
Steve Turner

FLORIDA
CHARLOTTE COUNTY (MURDOCK
CITY) (11)

laude Lemieux
lavid Longenecker
homas Lyttle
loris Mathis
Jesley Mearidy
acques Milhomme
harlene Miller
dna Minnis
ason Negm
fildred Nesmith
'wight Olmstead
faritza Pabon
unil Paul
orge Perdomo
eonard Poliandro
oci Ravelomanantsoa
onia Ridley
rthur Robinson
aul Robinson
enjamin Rodriguez
rederic Rosenstein
arlos Santos
errence Stroombeck
arol Tisdale
ary Uhlmann
ort Lauderdale Unknown
keleton Unknown
lollywood Unknown
fauricio Vindel
ames Weaver
.obert Weiby
erry Whipple
ames Wood
eon Woodward

T. MYERS (16)
louglas A.
uis A.
rian
ee D.
lennis
verett F.
.manda K.
laniel L.
.ndrew M.
ary M.

James P.
David S.
Daniel W.
Jason W.
Unknown Male

HUDSON (PASCO COUNTY) (8) (84)
52 men and 32 women
Dennis
Victor
Colleen

KEY WEST (11)

MELBOURNE (12)
Dennis Adams, 51
Donald Blair, 62
William Breeney, 48
Albert Gladue, 57
Nate Howes, 51
Loretta Johnson, 43
John Joseph King, 53
John Mertlik, 50
Susan Jean Odom, 51
John Tompkins, 52
Larry Walker, 62
Larry Whitaker, 61

MIAMI (MIAMI-DADE) (121)
Homeless and formerly homeless
Grisel Acosta, 39
Armando Aguilar, 50
Carlos Aguilar, 65
Edwin Alexander, 41
Antonio Alexis, 42
Ray "Alabama" Allen, 52
Rollanis Andino, 40
Mario Arguelles-Guerra, 47
Enio Ludese Augustin, 47
Timothy B., 48
Paulino Baker , 71
Ceril Baptiste, 56
Victor Bar elemy, 58
Ricardo Batista, 61
Judith Bertenshaw, 46
Jean Blaha, 85

Pedro Borroquez, 52
George C., 33
Danilo Cabrera, 54
Boris Chevchin, 70
Steven Childrey, 48
Mirian Cortaro, 60
Gloria Esther Cotto, 50
Ashley Devilliers, 41
Carlos Miguel Dorta, 54
Judith Eide, 52
Rafael Falcon, 76
Lazaro Delgago Fernandez, 47
Maribel Alicia Fonseca, 65
Daniel Garcia, 38
Eduardo Garcia, 71
Gerald Paul Gless, 35
Samuel Gomez-Rodriguez, 44
Alfredo Gonzalez, 43
Raynaldo Gonzalez, 61
Kenneth Gooding, 45
Benny Green, 49
Richard Grizzel, 65
Daniel Hardy, 47
Michael Harrington, 35
Kenneth Hart, 51
John Hawk, 47
Andres Hernandez, 65
Mario Hernandez, 59
Henry Hodge, 64
Ernest Holmes, 67
Robert Hoskins, 37
Richmond Hymes, 54
Lazaro Jimenez, 60
James Michael Jones, 58
Sandra Ann Kish, 64
Carlos L., 30
Augustin Lago, 58
Jose Linares, 56
Juan A. Llanes, 52
Soraya Lopez, 39
Carlos Martinez, 80
Estela Martinez, 43
Norberto Martinez, 68
Raul Martinez, 54
Keith McDuffy, 50
Elizabeth Jean McHugh, 42

Morgan John Thomas, 56
Francis Thompson, 56
John James "Killer" Thompson, 63
Otho Thorpe, 59
Alan Traitz, 54
Harvey Caton Turner, 47
Lazaro Vazquez, 64
Hector L. Velez, 50
Arturo Vera, 40
Salvador Verdecia, 54
Marie W., 50
Eric White, 60
Jessie Willis, 53

NAPLES (14)
Jeffery Brenner
Thomas Chapman
Billy Fisher
Donald Kitchell
Kevin Lowe
Tonya Martin
Jim McFall
John Moitie
Al Morris
Michel Paeth
Ted Pratico
Steve Skoguland
Clifford Vest
Daryl Williams

ORLANDO (25)
Paul Akin
"Cigar" Bill
Willis Deloach
Jeff Guncy
Debra Hardin
Barbara Hensley
Don Howard
Tony Landrum
Larry Lindsey
Jeffery Scott Maynard (a.k.a. "Jazz")
Robert Newton
Clarence Perkins
Ray Roberts
Robert Rosinski
Jim Shaw, early 40s

Pedro Medina, 67
Antonio Mendez, 55
(Infant Boy) Mohr
Lazaro Moreno, 47
Charles Morrell, 35
Anthony Muldrow, 48
Jeffrey Niccolls, 55
Tonya North, 38
Isidro Oliva, 50
Esterban Ortiz, 71
William A. Payne II, 54
Alberto Luis Perez, 58
Horacio Perez , 64
Justino Perez, 57
Grisel Perez, 52
Brian Peterson, 54
Martha Peterson, Infant
Donna Pevey, 49
Albert Principe, 56
Tomas Pruneda, 63
Jorge O. Puerta, 44
William Benjamin Quives, 6
Oscar R., 57
Allen Ray, 50
Eric August Reuther, 52
John Reyes, 50
Juan Rios, 47
David Bruce Robinson, 61
Eduardo Rodriguez, 70
Judith Rodriguez, 45
Pablo Rodriguez, 53
Pedro Rubalcaba, 64
Eugene Ruiz, 53
Randy Rushford, 67
Osvaldo Santiago, 52
Julio Sastre, 58
John Silipena, 50
Connie Simmons, 61
John Smith, Jr., 64
Aroldo Suarez, 83
German Suarez, 62
Angel Surdiadur, 61
Jerome Sydnor, 61
Dinora T., 51
Lisa Tedder, 37
Giovanni Thermidor, 18

Sharon Dancer
Arthur Davis
Regina Davis
Jesus Delatorre
Henry Diaz
Miguel Diaz
Douglas Dimas
Ruben Deanda
John Doe #03
John Doe #214
John Doe #260
Drew Drolshagen
Jose Duarte
Gerardo Encinas
Jonothan Enos
Guadalupe Estrada
Rudolpho Fajardo
John Farris
Lara Felix
Reynaldo Felix
Manuel Ferrales
Kelly Finan
Edward Fischer
Kerry Fisher
Edward Fitzgerald
James Fitzmaurice
Adam Flores
Anthony Foshee
Shirley Fresquez
Joel Frias Jr.
Jeffery Garcia
Ricky Garcia
Xavier Garcia
Ferdinand Gaspard III
Justin Gernannt
Shirly Gibson
David Gillian
Steve Gino
D'angelo Giovanni
Keith Glascoe
Francisco Gomez
Estevan Gonzalez
Gilbert Gonzalez
Nickey Gonzalez
Stanley Gordon
Larry Gore

Austin Brockman, 62
Roy G. Carter, 53
Danny Collins, 47
David Kasin, 41
Robert McCalley, 51
Danny Reta 46
David Siler, 49
Steven Winters, 50
3 United States Military Veterans:
Frank Ezzelle, 66
William Harrison, 57
Paul Mickiewicz, 48

FT. LAUDERDALE (BROWARD COUNTY) (65)
Maria Acevedo
Charles Bamberg
William Bennett
Karen Bradley
Patrick Brennan
Raymond Brewster
James Briscoe
Larry Brown
David Campbell
Alejandro Cardenas
Andrew Colias
Shamesa Conway
George Coppola
Donald Crockett
Alex Delrio
Jennie Dimitas
Earl Everett
James Fillicetti
Curtis Floyd
Lauren Forrester
Darwin Frazier
Casey Gibson
Christopher Granberg
Justine Gundersen
Douglas Hardin
John Helow
Darrol Henry
Timothy Jackson
Heleen Jay
Debra Johnson
Javier Kelly

Claude Lemeux
David Longenecker
Thomas Lythe
Denis Mathis
Wesley Meardy
Jacques Milhomme
Charlene Miller
Edna Minnis
Jason Negin
Mildred Nesmith
Dwight Olmstead
Maritza Pabon
Sunil Paul
Jorge Perdomo
Leonard Polundro
Loci Ravelomanantsoa
Tona Ridley
Arthur Robinson
Paul Robinson
Benjamin Rodriguez
Frederic Rosenstein
Carlos Santos
Terrence Stormbeck
Carol Tisdale
Gary Uhmann
Fort Lauderdale Unknown
Skeleton Unknown
Hollywood Unknown
Mauricio Vitobi
James Werner
Robert Welby
Terry Whipple
James Wood
Leon Woodward

FT. MYERS (16)
Douglas A.
Luis A.
Brian
Lee D.
Dennis
Everett F.
Amanda K.
Daniel L.
Andrew M.
Gary M.

James P.
David S.
Daniel W.
Jason W.
Unknown Male

HUDSON (PASCO COUNTY) (84)
52 men and 32 women
Dennis
Victor
Colleen

KEY WEST (11)

MELBOURNE (12)
Dennis Adams, 51
Donald Blair, 62
William Breeney, 48
Albert Gladue, 57
Nate Howes, 51
Loretta Johnson, 43
John Joseph King, 53
John Mertlik, 50
Susan Jean Odom, 51
John Tompkins, 52
Larry Walker, 62
Larry Whitaker, 61

MIAMI (MIAMI-DADE) (121)
Homeless and formerly homeless
Grisel Acosta, 39
Armando Aguilar, 50
Carlos Aguilar, 65
Edwin Alexander, 41
Antonio Alexis, 42
Ray "Alabama" Allen, 52
Rollanis Andino, 40
Mario Arguelles-Guerra, 47
Enio Ludese Augustin, 47
Timothy B., 48
Paulino Baker , 71
Ceril Baptiste, 56
Victor Bar eleury, 58
Ricardo Batista, 61
Judith Bertenshaw, 46
Jean Blaha, 85

James P.
David S.
Daniel W.
Jason W.
Unknown Male

HUDSON (PASCO COUNTY) (84)
52 men and 32 women
Dennis
Victor
Colleen

KEY WEST (11)

MELBOURNE (12)
Dennis Adams, 51
Donald Blair, 62
William Breeney, 48
Albert Gladne, 57
Nate Howes, 51
Loretta Johnson, 45
John Joseph King, 53
John Merlik, 59
Susan Jean Odom, 51
John Tompkins, 52
Larry Walker, 62
Larry Whitaker, 61

MIAMI (MIAMI-DADE) (121)
Homeless and formerly homeless
Grisel Acosta, 39
Amando Aguilar, 50
Carlos Aguilar, 65
Edwin Alexander, 41
Antonio Alexis, 42
Ray "Alabama" Allen, 52
Robinsu Andino, 40
Mario Arguelles-Guerra, 47
Enio Luciene Augustin, 47
Timothy B., 48
Paulino Baker, 71
Cecil Baptiste, 56
Victor Bar eleony, 58
Ricardo Batista, 61
Judith Bertenshaw, 46
Jean Blaha, 85

Pedro Bravoperez, 52
George C., 35
Danilo Cabrera, 54
Boris Caevcinir, 70
Steven Childrey, 40
Miriam Cordero, 60
Gloria Esther Cotto, 50
Ashley Devilliers, 41
Carlos Miguel Docta, 54
Judith Estle, 52
Rafael Falcon, 76
Lazaro Delepsio Fernandez, 47
Maribel Alina Fonseca, 65
Daniel Garcia, 58
Eduardo Garcia, 71
Gerald Paul Glew, 55
Samuel Gomez-Rodriguez, 44
Alfredo Gonzalez, 43
Reynaldo Gonzalez, 61
Kenneth Gooding, 45
Benny Green, 49
Richard Grizas, 65
Daniel Hardy, 47
Michael Harrington, 55
Kenneth Hart, 51
John Hawk, 67
Andres Hernandez, 65
Mario Hernandez, 59
Henry Hodge, 64
Ernest Holston, 67
Robert Hoskins, 37
Richmond Hynne, 54
Lazaro Jimenez, 60
James Michael Jones, 58
Sandra Ann Kirk, 84
Carlos L., 30
Augustin Lago, 58
Jose Linares, 36
Juan A. Llanes, 52
Soreyo Lopez, 39
Carlos Martinez, 80
Estela Martinez, 42
Norberto Martinez, 68
Raul Martinez, 64
Keith McDuffy, 50
Elizabeth Jean McHugh, 42

Pedro Medina, 67
Antonio Mendez, 55
(Infant Boy) Mohr
Lazaro Moreno, 47
Charles Morrell, 35
Anthony Muldrow, 48
Jeffrey Niccolls, 55
Tonya North, 38
Isidro Oliva, 50
Esterban Ortiz, 71
William A. Payne II, 54
Alberto Luis Perez, 58
Horacio Perez , 64
Justino Perez, 57
Grisel Perez, 52
Brian Peterson, 54
Martha Peterson, Infant
Donna Pevey, 49
Albert Principe, 56
Tomas Pruneda, 63
Jorge O. Puerta, 44
William Benjamin Quives, (
Oscar R., 57
Allen Ray, 50
Eric August Reuther, 52
John Reyes, 50
Juan Rios, 47
David Bruce Robinson, 61
Eduardo Rodriguez, 70
Judith Rodriguez, 45
Pablo Rodriguez, 53
Pedro Rubalcaba, 64
Eugene Ruiz, 53
Randy Rushford, 67
Osvaldo Santiago, 52
Julio Sastre, 58
John Silipena, 50
Connie Simmons, 61
John Smith, Jr., 64
Aroldo Suarez, 83
German Suarez, 62
Angel Surdiadur, 61
Jerome Sydnor, 61
Dinora T., 51
Lisa Tedder, 37
Giovanni Thermidor, 18

Morgan John Thomas, 56
Francis Thompson, 56
John James "Killer" Thompson, 63
Otho Thorpe, 59
Alan Traitz, 54
Harvey Caton Turner, 47
Lazaro Vazquez, 64
Hector L. Velez, 50
Arturo Vera, 40
Salvador Verdecia, 54
Marie W., 50
Eric White, 60
Jessie Willis, 53

NAPLES (14)
Jeffery Bremer
Thomas Chapman
Billy Fisher
Donald Kitchell
Kevin Lowe
Tonya Martin
Jim McFall
John Mosbe
Al Morris
Michel Paeth
Ted Pratico
Steve Skogsland
Clifford Vest
Daryl Williams

ORLANDO (25)
Paul Akin
"Cigar" Bill
Willis Deloach
Jeff Gracey
Debra Hardin
Barbara Hensley
Don Howard
Tony Landrum
Larry Lindsey
Jeffery Scott Maynard (a.k.a. "Jazz"
Robert Newton
Clarence Perkins
Ray Roberts
Robert Rosinski
Jim Shaw, early 40s

Clarence Snyder
Brenda Sumner, 49
Michael Szweda
Jerry Thomas
Bruce Warness
Katie White
Richard White
Marilyn Woods, 55
Anonymous Male (hit by car)
Anonymous Male (killed in homeless camp)

PINELLAS (22)
Marshall Bailey
Bennie
Bobby Bureston
Eli
John Garrett
William Gillespie
Craig Kennedy
Ken Kirstis
Paul Knapp
Mark Lafferty
Fawn Muholland
James Mitcham
Lisa Parker
Diana Rasheed
Joseph Rivera
Neve Shantai
Kimberly Stewart
Jeremiah Tebidow
Alberto Vargas
Raymund Villiall
David Watford
Estelle Yurman

TALLAHASSEE
Organizers have chosen not to release names.

TAMPA (53)
Roy Olan Ashby, 43
Willie Bass, 42
Russell Beagle, 56
Kathy Bellamy, 53
William Browder, 57

Serenity Brown, 1 month
Leonard Carlson, 55
Gregory Cogan, 52
Noe Cruz, 39
Donald Day, 44
William Elberdt, 55
Ronald Embree, 52
Keith Ezzell, 50
William George, 32
William Gregory, 57
Ray Hagedorn, 62
Marc Harvard, 61
Robert Hutlenloch, 59
Donald "Shaggy" Kay, 44
Willie Key, 66
Larry Leggett, 48
Raphael Lopez, 28
Frank MacLaughlin, 66
Ronnie McDaniel, 61
Thomas Mobley, 47
Barbara Mongere, 51
Michael Ortega, 47
Pedro Ortiz, 60
Dennis Pogorsky, 52
Johnnie Ree, unknown
Robert Ryan, 27
Douglas Samec, 45
Isaac Santiago, 66
Eduardo Santos, 63
Wanda Scott, 44
Jalkiz Segura-Gonzalez, 59
Howard Short, 44
Nancy Smith, 46
Clifford Spears, 49
John Swenson, 61
Andrea Tolliver, 39
Rafael Torres, 51
Lawrence Wallace, 60
Debra Wagner, 46
Kendall Waters, 41
Radell Wilcox, 52
Harold, unknown
Wanda, early 40s
Wanda, unknown
Unidentified Male, 52
Unidentified Female, age unknown

James Slinger
Sharon Souza
Robert D. Starr
Kenneth Stewart
Timothy Aaron Stovall
Todd Strebe
Ronald Irwin Studer
Michael Raymond Taylor
David Robert Thomas
David A. Tomlinson
Ba Van Trang
Antonio Valdez
Terry Valladao
Bulmaro Valladarez, Jr.
Daniel Van Kethlan
Felix Villalba, Jr.
Marta Warner
Thomas White

Individuals who died in transitional or permanent housing for the formerly homeless (16):
Joe Barfield
Dorothy Burrow
Chris Chase
Cornell Conley
Oscar Franco
Henry Houghton
May Jimenez
Ron Kerr
Beverly Nesbit
Van Nguyen
John Sanchez
Richard Stasi
Brad Sullivan
Star Thiebaud
William Vaughn
Ruby White

SANTA CRUZ (33)
Homeless and formerly homeless
Mickey "Mickey Joseph" Allen, 43
Patrick Ball, 54
Richard Barrett, 56
Colt Behler, 39

Toma Cole, 52
Dean Drew, 58
Kenneth "Curly" Edwards, 67
Andrew John Fitts, 48
Jeremy "Jeremy Ward" French, 44
Crystal Goble, 51
Terry Grennan, 52
Roberto Hernandez, 51
Christopher Hutchinson, 35
James "Boston" Leonard, 44
Thomas Vernon Lewis, 50
Timothy Maguire, 49
William Manns, 42
Roger McGary, 43
John Nestler, 52
Daniel "Dan" Oas, 57
Michael O'Neil, 61
Trinidad "Miguel" Perez, 61
Anthony Perez, 52
Margarita Peters, 54
Gilbert "Gabby" Ramirez, 46
Salvador Ramirez, 49
Michael Eugene Rinaldi, 51
Bradley Robinson, 40
Linda Santean, 49
Michael "Stoney" Trantham, 53
Suzanne Turner, 62
John "John Earth" Widell, 64
Joel Wood, 57

VENTURA (20)
Donald Archer, 48
Kevin Asuncion, 37
Kenneth Barlow, 34
James Beck, age unknown
Serafin Bostello, 43
Rob Roy Brown, 34
Dwayne Gillespie, 59
Jacob Henry, 26
Roy Kahn, 67
James Lannon, 31
Deanna Mason, 52
Cheryl Mayberry, 58
Michael Montero, age unknown
Raymond Nasser, age unknown
Richard Newton, 37

James Slinger
Sharon Souza
Robert D. Starr
Kenneth Stewart
Timothy Aaron Stovall
Todd Strebe
Ronald Erwin Studer
Michael Raymond Taylor
David Robert Thomas
David A. Tomlinson
Bu Van Trang
Antonio Valdez
Terry Valladao
Bulmaro Valladarez, Jr
Daniel Van Kelsas
Felix Villalba, Jr
Marta Warner
Thomas White

Individuals who died in
transitional or permanent
housing for the formerly
homeless (15):
Joe Barfield
Dorothy Burrow
Chris Chase
Cornell Conley
Oscar Franco
Henry Houghton
May Jimenez
Ron Kerr
Beverly Nesbit
Van Nguyen
John Sanchez
Richard Sessi
Brad Sullivan
Star Thiebaud
William Vaughn
Ruby White

SANTA CRUZ (33)
Homeless and formerly homeless
Mickey "Mickey Joseph" Allen, 43
Patrick Ball, 54
Richard Barnett, 56
Colt Bethke, 39

Tonia Cole, 52
Dean Drew, 58
Kenneth "Curly" Edwards, 67
Andrew John Fitts, 48
Jeremy "Jeremy Ward" French, 44
Crystal Goble, 51
Terry Greenan, 52
Roberto Hernandez, 51
Christopher Hutchison, 35
James "Bootsie" Leonard, 44
Thomas Vernon Lewis, 50
Timothy Maguire, 49
William Manns, 42
Roger McGary, 43
John Nestler, 52
Daniel "Dan" Oss, 57
Michael O'Neil, 61
Trinidad "Miguel" Perez, 61
Anthony Perez, 52
Margarita Peters, 54
Gilbert "Gabby" Ramirez, 46
Salvador Ramirez, 49
Michael Eugene Rinaldi, 51
Bradley Robinson, 40
Linda Santoni, 49
Michael "Stoney" Trantham, 53
Suzanne Turner, 62
John "John Earth" Widell, 64
Joel Wood, 37

VENTURA (20)
Donald Archer, 48
Kevin Asuncion, 37
Kenneth Barlow, 54
James Beck, age unknown
Serafin Bostello, 43
Rob Roy Brown, 54
Dwayne Gillespie, 59
Jacob Henry, 26
Roy Kahn, 67
James Larman, 51
Deanna Mason, 52
Cheryl Marberry, 58
Michael Montero, age unknown
Raymond Nasser, age unknown
Richard Newton, 37

Unidentified Male, age unknown
Unidentified Male, age unknown

WEST PALM BEACH (14)
Curtis Almareles (veteran)
Jose Arius, 41
Shelton Danzler (veteran)
Wendy Dunn, 39
Karl G.
Kenneth Gilpin
Phillip Graham, 43
William Johnson, 54
David Allen King
Rolondo Longoria, 27
Keith Rocillo, 33
Donald K. Thomas
Thomas Treharn, 58
David Ulmer, 41

GEORGIA
ATLANTA (42)
Otis Archie
Henry Asbey
Tony Bailey
Willie Bailey, Jr.
Jerry Barlow
Michael Barlow
Michael Bell
Roy Bell
Joseph Burke
Dominic Capone
Rose Carlisle
George Christian
Frederick Corkern
Mary Curry
James Daniels
Remona Dortch
Grady Edwards
Larry Elrod
David Floyd
Brenda Hampton
Sylvester Hawthorne
Emmett Huggins
Joe Huggins
Betty James
Carolyn Kilgore

Geraldine Lee
Gregory Lee
Willie Lee
Richard McWhorter
Cleavon Moore
Calvin Oliver
Russell Pink
Darryl Roberson
Layne Rose
Charles Smith
Frank Vuittonet
Joseph Walkes
Avia Williams
Byron Williams
Cynthia Woods
Timothy Young

ILLINOIS
CHICAGO (14)
Glenn
Leonard
Pamela
Ralph
Robert
Teresa
Wanda

ROCKFORD (12)
John C., 36
Nathan C., 29
Robert C., 37
Victoria C., 27
Jackie F., 47
Thomas H., 40
Beth L., 39
Gregory P., 34
David S., 47
Carneal W., 25
Linda W., 60
Evmorphia Z., 37

INDIANA
EVANSVILLE (6)
Jimmy Ray Chastain
Steve Durden
James Gordon, 41

NATIONAL HOME   L DAY MANUAL

James Hammel
Harrison Horne, 51
Joe Love

INDIANAPOLIS (38)
Scott Brewster, 59
John Burton
Robert Campher
Brad "Tree" Colema
Albert Wayne Colli
Kimberly Critchfiel
Clyde Delph
Joseph Domer
David Dullen
Jerry Edwards
Vernon Evans
Ron Fesler
Dale Foley
Terry Harlan
Marci Howard, 44
Robert Jenkins, 58
Reva Kelley
Allen Lee
Jack Lewis, 51
Wilbur Lewis
Clayton Lowery
Alphonso McFolley
Randolph McGowar
Kerry Rex McKee
Ernie Nevers
Jacqueline Ogden
Monica Peterson
Larry Powell
Victor (Simon) Ricl
Ron Rutland
Earl W. Scaife
David Ronald Scube
Douglas Snyder
Daniel Joe Trivett
William "Perry" Tro
Tony Williams, 40
David Woolfe
Michael Wolff

KOKOMO (27)
J. B., 50

The names of those honored were
not read at the service in preference
of a moment of silence.

PORTLAND (21)
The first names of those who died
were read at the vigil, but organizers
decided not to release the names for
publication.

MARYLAND
BALTIMORE (4)
From Franklin Square Hospital
event.
George D.
Cynthia H.
James E.
Marc H.
Julia L.
Charlotte S.
Levi S.
Brian Z.

MASSACHUSETTS
WORCESTER (7)
Ruby E. (Marci) Schippers
Nancy

MICHIGAN
TRAVERSE CITY (19)
Harry Armstrong
Scott Redlang
Nancy Chambers
Harry Chastnet
Christopher Davidson
James G.
Betty Grochowalski
Steve Gunn
Wayne Jack
Kat
Thomas Kang
Dale Kuhn
Joel Niedjielski
Edry Parcher-Gablow
James Schooley
Lee Scott

KANSAS
WICHITA (3)

KENTUCKY
LEXINGTON-FAYETTE
Honored were 21 people who were
currently homeless or had been
touched by homelessness at some
point.

LOUISIANA
NEW ORLEANS (10)

MAINE
BANGOR (6)
LEWISTON

MINNESOTA
DULUTH (1
Carla Bingle
Steven Bart
Johnny Mo
Allen Webb

MINNEAPOI
People from
Faribault, E
Maple Plan
Rochester, I
Owatonna,
Minnetonka
Minneapoli
Billie Amaro
Rosemary F
Leyton Ash
Thomas Bel
Verrall Bor
Bruce Berp
Anthony Bo
Colleen Ma
Ruby D. Bo
Michael Bo
Marcus Jam
Michael Le
Kim Engers
Jimmy Lee
Gerald Coll
Mark Derri
Sharon Lee
Luanyo Alc
Doris A. D
Andrew Ke
Troy Gerra
Nicholas Sc
Charles Hal
Vincent Hal
William Le
Michael Ed
Marilyn Fry

David Saal
Stanley Wo
Charles Zur

THE FIRST DAY OF THE FIRST DAY OF WINTER, THE LONGEST NIGHT OF THE YEAR. HT OF THE YEAR.

101

The names of those honored were not read at the service in preference of a moment of silence.

PORTLAND (21)
The first names of those who died were read at the vigil, but organizers decided not to release the names for publication.

MARYLAND
BALTIMORE (47)
From Franklin Square Hospital event.
George D.
Cynthia F.
James H.
Marc H.
John L.
Charlotte S.
Levi S.
Brian Z.

MASSACHUSETTS
WORCESTER (7)
Ruby E. (Mimi) Schippers
Nancy

MICHIGAN
TRAVERSE CITY (19)
Harry Armstrong
Scott Belling
Nancy Chambers
Harry Chestnut
Christopher Davidson
James G.
Betty Grochowalski
Steve Gunn
Wayne Jack
Kat
Thomas King
Dale Kuhn
Joel Niedjelski
Edy Prucker-Goblow
Janet Schooley
Lee Scott

David Small
Stanley Woods
Charles Zimmerah

MINNESOTA
DULUTH (12)
Carla Bagley
Steven Baxter
Johnny Moore
Allan Webb

MINNEAPOLIS (130)
People from Anoka, Carleton, Duluth, Faribault, Fridley, Hennepin City, Maple Plain, Minneapolis, Mankato, Rochester, Red Wing, St. Paul, Owatonna, St. Louis Park & Minnetonka were honored at the Minneapolis Service
Billie Amos
Rosemary Pauline Anderson, 50
Layton Ashley, 55
Thomas Baker, 39
Verzell Burnett, 54
Bruce Bergquist, 50
Anthony Bogar, 48
Colleen Mary Brophey, 59
Ruby D. Bryant, 37
Michael Buchanan, 54
Marcus James Burrell, 38
Michael Lee Chavez, 50
Kim Eugene Clark, 34
Jimmy Lee Coleman, 55
Gerald Collier, 49
Mark Detrick
Sharon Lee Drumbeater Voss, 39
Luanyo Alonso Dumegi, 52
Doris A. DuBois, 45
Andrew Kevin Fierro, 43
Troy Gervais, 35
Nicholas Scott Gustafson, 23
Charles Hall, 57
Vincent Hillier, 47
William Lee Handler, 55
Michael Edward Herron, 55
Marilyn Fay Howard, 46

Rosalie McGaughey
John McGraham
Charles McLain
Edis McNeil
David McRobie, Jr
Miguel Mejia
Gerardo Mendez
Jorge Mendez
Erminda Mendoza
Todd Michalski
Ronda Miles
Jerry Miller
Joseph Miller
Manuel Miranda
Mohammad
Humberto Monteaguido
Jesse Moore
Nathan Morgan
Lyn Moss
Gabriel Moya
Mark Moyer
Gary Myers
Alajos Nagy
Frederick Neumeier
Nhon Nguyen
Michael Nichols
Francisco Nieves
Stacy Norton
William Nowling
Marian Ocampo
Noel Ocampo
Candice Ogan
Mamerto Orantes
Tansley Orndge
Manuel Orozco
Mary Oswald
Curtis Owen
Anthony Padilla
Miguel Padilla
Ricardo Palafox
Jose Urcuyo Paramo
Maximiliano Pasaye
Jeffrey Patrick
Ion Pena
Margarita Perez
Ralph Perez

Shawn Pettway
Vernon Phillips
William Pickens
Kevin Pierce
Jerry Pina
Victor Pineda
George Pirylis
Andres Gonzalez Porta
Julie Potter
Preston Pringle
Laurie Pruett
Louis Quimiro
Manuel Ramirez
Jesse Ramirez
Pedro Ramirez
Narciso Ramos
Phillip Ramos, Jr.
Sandra Randolph
Jaime Rangel
Luther Ray
Raymundo
Virginia Refai
Severo Reyes
Virginia Rialls
Lori Roberson
Brenda Roberts
Ray Robertson
Kevin Robinson
Barbara Rodriguez
Rafael Rosales
Frank Rosen
Robert Russell
Keith Sabin
Leonardo Salas
Maurilio Saldana
Sangmas Saluckait
Mario Sanchez
Raphael Sanchez
Richard Santos
Stacey Schwann
Jean Sciabbarrasi
Eddie Scott
Scott Segobiano
William Seward
Danny Shields
Hamid Shraufat

Emmett James Smith, 59
Robert Sougart, 59
Kenneth Tyrell
Troy Richard Ulrich, 42
John Ward, 58
Reginald "Reggie" Washington, 51
Kenneth Weasner, 60
"Chief" Dick Whitcomb
Andrew Lee Wilbert, 61
Daniel Wohlfiel, 56
Robert "Angel" Zygulinski, 62
Delima
Judy, 64

Advocates:
Kelly Andrews, 27
Mary Bird, 60
Greg Horan, 60
Mohamed Issa, 30
Pat Kline
Cliff Woodie, 60

RED LAKE
Organizers have chosen not to
release names.

MISSOURI

St. Joseph (3)
Female
Male, 52
Male, 54

St. Louis (30)
Paula Armstead
Michael Ballard
Lonnie Butler
John Bell
Emma Bine
Elvis Boyette
Jeremy Dunlap
Benjamin Gardner
Dennis Harris
Carl Hodge
Crystal Hodges
Donna Holiday
Dennis Kettsimer

Smith, 59
Mack Lape, 59
Terri Laut,
Terrell McClosk, 42
Clarice "T
Lou Pfeiffer Washington, 51
Edward Polk, 60
Randy Puff Richmond
Andrew Rudiert, 61
William Sel, 56
Uninco Sau Zygulinski, 62
Wesley Th
John Todd
Tony Tura
Belinda W
David Will, 27
Al William
Michael, W,
t, 50

MONTANA (29)
HELENA (80)

NEBRASKA
OMAHA (# chosen not to
Herman Ev
Harold "Po
Ezekiel Be
Richard Big
Frances "F
Vinnie Boo
Janelle Bro
Brian Buzn
Jennie Dun
Lori Clark,
Rodney Da,
Allen Dun
Terry Falk
Christine C
Jeffrey Ha
Mark Hanz
Ben Hoer,
Dennis Ho
Robert Hu
Kathleen J,
Coma And
Patrick Jes
Beryl Kish

Matt Lepsua
Terri Lawrence
Terrell Mosley
Clarice "Ta" Morton
Lou Pfeiffer
Edward Pollan
Randy Pollan
Andrew Rueckerf
William Sellner
Vance Smith
Wesley Thomas
John Todd
Tony Turner
Belinda Walls
David Wilkins
Al Williams
Michael Williams

MONTANA (29)
HELENA (1)

NEBRASKA
OMAHA (40)
Herman Bell, 65
Harold "Papa Sandf" Berger, 62
Ezekiel Berry, 21 months
Richard Bjorklund, 36
Frances "Frankie" Briggs, 46
Vinnie Boccia, 64
Janelle Browning, 45
Brian Bundy, 34
Jennie Diamond, 30
Lori Clark, 46
Rodney Deville, 51
Allan Dunn, 43
Terry ritlike, age unknown
Christine Grohausner, age unknown
Jeffrey Hartman, 43
Mark Hinch, 47
Ben Hoer, 72
Dennis Howard, 46
Robert Hirst, age unknown
Kathleen Jackson, age unknown
Coma Jacobson, 29
Patrick James, 44
Beryl Kishnum, 62

Pete Luman, 64
Kevin Lonewolf, 45
Bobbie McGee, 57
Marshall Nelson, 40s
Manual Pacheco, 46
Myles Ross, 27
Jeff Schaefer, age unknown
Wade Seestrem, 44
Richie Seils, age unknown
Jim Tamonet, 57
Timothy Torske, 57
Anthony White, 50s
Eric Wilk, 53
Louise Witte, 48
Alex Williams, 45
Harry Wippner, 45
Don Younger, 39

NEVADA
LAS VEGAS (50)
Tragoye Legasse Abdi, 36
Brian Gregory Anderson, 23
Don Dee Astorga, 39
John Austin, 41
Roberto Ayala, 57
Thomas Jefferson Bell, Jr., 81
Austin T Bishop, 78
Jocelyn Burroman, 48
William R Brownsall, 44
Twila Naomi Cline, 57
Jack Dudley Cock, 55
Mack Corsikem, 51
Pedro O. Cordovo, 49
Francisco Diaz, 38
John Doe "Desert Lot", age
unknown
Thomas W. Duncan, 59
Richard Lee Fish, 55
John Joseph Harden, 70
Steven Wayne Hatchery, 48
Gary William Johnston, 56
George Kingston, 54
Gregg Kohr, 45
Kenneth Krul, 57
William Arthur Repke, 22
Cora Angie Low, 63

Noman
Lout 3
Alton E
Arron A
Andrew
Eldpio C
Darren '
Gabriel
Sergio C
John D
James F
Kasuel
Kathlee
Paul Mi
Robert,
Richard
Michael
Fred W
Antoine
Edward
Paul Ja
Curtis L
Anthony
David J
Eliezer

NEW HAMPS
CLARE
LACON
& NAS
Steve
Micha
Josep
Willis
Greg
Susan
Robin
Gary
Ray "
Rosha
Gail E
Denis
Janet
Chris
Katrin
Roger

Pete Laura, 64
Kevin Lonewolf, 43
Bobbie McGee, 57
Marshall Nelson, 40s
Manual Pacheco, 46
Myles Ross, 27
Jeff Schultz, age unknown
Wade Seidman, 44
Rickie Solis, age unknown
Jim Fontaine, 57
Timothy Tarcha, 57
Anthony White, 50s
Eric Wilt, 53
Leana Witte, 48
Alex Williams, 49
Harry Wippert, 46
Don Younger, 39

NEVADA

LAS VEGAS (60)
Teegyve Legenie Abdi, 36
Brian Gregory Anderson, 23
Don Dee Astorga, 29
John Austin, 47
Roberto Ayala, 37
Thomas Jefferson Bell, Jr., 61
Austin T. Bishop, 78
Jocelyn Bezrouses, 48
William R. Brownell, 44
Twila Naomi Cline, 57
Jack Dudley Cook, 55
Mark Cordero, 51
Pedro O. Cordova, 49
Francisco Diaz, 38
John Doe "Desert Lot", age unknown
Thomas W. Duncan, 59
Richard Lee Frith, 55
John Joseph Hersher, 70
Steven Wayne Humphry, 43
Gary William Johnston, 56
George Kingston, 54
Gregg Kolar, 45
Kenneth Krol, 57
William Arthur Kuplic, 22
Cen Angie Low, 65

Norman Avery Mabry, 38
Louis Martin Maser, 50
Alton Edwin McClellan, 46
Aaron A. McCorias, Jr., 30
Andrew James Mueller, 54
Eligio Ortega, 26
Darren W. Plunk, 34
Gabriel Provence, 47
Sergio Quezeda, 36
John D. Quinn, 49
James Ronaroncas, Jr., 52
Kenneth Reeves, 44
Kathleen M. Sargent, 54
Paul Michael Schaffer, 54
Robert Scott Searcy, 19
Richard Edward Stanley, 43
Michael Francis Sternberg, 59
Fred William Tunnicliff, 49
Antwaun Vargas, 36
Eduardo Velazquez, 26
Paul James Vietor, 55
Curtis L. Williams, 44
Anthony Wooten, 37
David Joseph Yob, 52
Eliezer Zamora, 29

NEW HAMPSHIRE

CLAREMONT, CONCORD, KEENE, LACONIA, LEBANON, MANCHESTER & NASHUA (19)
Steve Aliberti (Concord?)
Michelle Bernard
Joseph Carignan (Manchester)
William Dupuis
Greg Jette
Susan K.
Robin Kulingeskn
Gary LeLievre
Ray "Beaux" Leoma (Concord)
Richard "Dickie" McKinley
Gail Paquette
Denise Pena
Janet Perreault
Chris Purdy
Kenneth Richer (Manchester)
Roger "Shorty" Rondeau

Bob Sayed
Albert Summerlin
Vernon
Carl Vickroy
Jesse Whigham
William
Demetrius Wood

CLEVELAND (50)
Olu Akintunde
Anonymous
Charles D. Anderson
John Andresh
Ronald Armstrong
Cliff Barnhart
Rosemary Battle
Terry Beachman
Paul Bianco
Jacob Bobrowski
Robert Cherney
James Cofield
Ralph Duhan
Robert Eady
Barney Elias
Carol Fergus
Larry Gahan
Jacinda Glover
Carol Good (male)
Jack Hanrahan
Jesse Harris
Gary Hubbard
Joseph Irby
Thomas Jackson
James King Jr.
James King
Perry Kucinich
Rufuss Lenard
Mariam Lozada
Craig Lucas
Marnie Macon
Marion McWilliams
Thomas Milo
Robert Morgan
Bruce Morris
Mary Murphy
Melvin Nance

Bob Sayed
Albert Summerlin
Vernon
Carl Vickroy
Jesse Whigham
William
Demetrius Wood

CLEVELAND (50)
Olu Akintunde
Anonymous
Charles D. Anderson
John Andresh
Ronald Armstrong
Cliff Barnhart
Rosemary Battle
Terry Beachman
Paul Bianco
Jacob Bobrowski
Robert Cherney
James Cofield
Ralph Duhan
Robert Eady
Barney Elias
Carol Fergus
Larry Gahan
Jacinda Glover
Carol Good (male)
Jack Hanrahan
Jesse Harris
Gary Hubbard
Joseph Irby
Thomas Jackson
James King Jr.
James King
Perry Kucinich
Rufuss Lenard
Mariam Lozada
Craig Lucas
Marnie Macon
Marion McWilliams
Thomas Milo
Robert Morgan
Bruce Morris
Mary Murphy
Melvin Nance

Robert Okragley
Donald O'Neal
John Pickell
Stanley Pieck
Mark Pirtle
Thomas Rapose
Barbara Rossi
Calvin Sledge
Jeff Stoudemire
Lois Swaysland
Wayne Anthony Tyler
Anthony Waters
William Whalen

COLUMBUS (36)
Christopher Adams
Gabriel Arnn
Jerome Bannister
Eric Blakey
Kevin Bryant
Tracey Burgess
David Cornwell
David H. DeVore
Alonzo Dowdy
Violet Daisy Edwards
Kenneth Freed
Arnold Gray
Renee Hickey
Jimmy Edward Hicks
Thomas S. Hill
James Kuisel Jr.
Robert Leitwein
Eva Lowery
Moses Nixon
Levie Peoples
Robert L. Phipps, Jr.
Beloved Quail
Clay Rinearson
Cynthia Ross
Mark Sanders
Ricky Sidders
James Skag
Antonio Stith
Robert Stump
Trent T.
Max Turley

Vivian Vance
Wendell Ward
Ralph Welham
Larry D. Wesley
Jack Woodward

DAYTON (19)
Adam, 50
Barchan, 49
Blaz, 51
Bobby, 56
Casey, 28
Christopher, 43
Eugene, 53
Floyd, 57
Gary, 51
Gregory, 57
James, 54
Jeff; age unknown
Julia 43
Marquish, 54
Maurice, 49
Ocie, 52
Phillip, 49
Scott, 38
Shon, 51

PENNSYLVANIA
PHILADELPHIA (65)
Americus Leroy Johnson
Shirley Domurak
Jeffrey LaVoe
Howard Jackson
Yancy Smith

RHODE ISLAND
PROVIDENCE (18+)
Walter Bennett
Montue Bonante
Robert D'Ambra
Diane Denoier
Chris Diehl
Karen Holloway
Jim Keaveney
Armand Landry
Paul Langlois

John Miller
Carlton Bruce Newkirk
Dominic Poole
Bob Pangborn
Nikolaas Claire Pearson
Steve Perry
David Raymund
David E. Spears
Billy Spencer
Peter Silva
Chris Thwent
Donald Wall
Jeff Wells
William Matthew Wilde
"Flippie George"
Bobby J
Matt
Chris
Branch
"Chief"
"Chimaboa"
"Sparky"

SOUTH CAROLINA
CHARLESTON (9)
Elizabeth Bingley, 52
Wallace Blome, 58
Naikeda Bright, 35
Douglas Collier, 44
Kerry Moore 51
John Powders, 61
Billy Rogers, 36
Anita Tilton, 70
Herbert Tyler, 62

TENNESSEE
MEMPHIS (36)
Dean Alex
Barry Anderson
Donald Bradshaw
Melvin Brakins
Aaron Cherry
Ron Cowen
Frank Douglas
Casey Elder
Mike Farrish

1

Jerry Garret
Gary Heinze
George Huggins
James Hodge
Ronald Joe
Kevin Jones
Little John Lumpkin
Deborah Martin
Natalie Mason
Ernest Milligan
Herbert Mitchell
Frank Mitchner
Solin "White Country" Nails
Terry Nauer
Anthony Robinson
Raymond Robinson
Rodney "at Cooper and Centra
Jessie Sanford
Bob Van Camp
Mary Washington
Gloria Williams

NASHVILLE (37)
Bruce Edward A.
Larry Gilbert B.
Jimmie Barrett
Charles Boritchard
Robert Darrell C.
Roy C.
James E. Calwell
Burnell Cotton
Terrance Demonbreun
Cyndi Demuth
Arthur Van F.
Harry Van F.
John Frederick F.
Dennis Lee G.
Dennis Gill
Victor Gonzoles
Ronald Ray Hendrick
Frank William M.
Jerry Dewayne M.
James McClelin
Latisha Miliken
Greg Mobly
Duke Patten

Walker Dee R., Jr.
Ed S.
Joseph S.
Joe Sheridan
Albert Silva
Solja
Billy Vond T.
John Patrick T.
Darryl Thomas
Darrel Thomspon
Jessie Tucker
Farris Vaughner
John Doe
John Doe

TEXAS

AUSTIN (135)
Jimmie Adams
Juntae Alex
Salvatore Aquilino
Juan Astran
Lois Atkinson
William Augustine
Cruz Avila
Royce Baker
Terry Barker
Christopher Barrow
Wylie Bennett, Jr.
Charles Biner
Archie "Chief" Blackowl
Eleanor Bolden
Joseph Bolduc
Patsy Bright
Chris Briley
Ramon Briones
Valerie Brook
Delover Bryant
James Burgess
Mark Butler
Charles Byrd
Steven Campbell
Margaret Canales
Mike Candelas
Martin Cantu
Ignacio Carrasco
Robert Carter

Billy Cave
Larry Cawvey
Marina Cazares
Robert Chenoweth
Levier Clifton
Donald Coffman
Alfred Coleman
Ray Cordova
Richelle Cowen
Michael Curtin
Carlester Davis
Mary Dixon
James Ellis
Sam Fairchild
Hector Figueroa
Billy Forrest
Mary Friend-Morgan
Robert Garcia
Amalia Garcia
Miguel Garza
Arthur Gonzales
Odelia Gonzales
James Gonzales
San Juanita Granada
James Griggs
Carson Hamblen
Anthony Harris
Carol Hart
Juan Hernandez
Mary Hight
Oscar Hotz
Walter Howard
Bennie Hunter
John Jackson
Kenneth James
Vernon Jefferson
Mary Johnson
Dometa Jones
Hung Kee
Eddie Kyser
John Lambert
Paul Larremore
Leslie Larrew
Melvin Legendre
Hope Leonard
Elza Levasseur

uan Ligues
Gregory Lipka
herry Mason
velyn McCartney
Villie McDade
esse McFarlan
utimio Mendoza
ack Miller
larbara Mitchell
tuart Montgomery
lijah Myers
trandon Newsome, Jr.
oseph North
immie Olvera
eola Peoples
ohn Perry, Jr.
aura Price
hirley Puckett
raci Quacker
amuel Rang
Iautie Reese
ndelko Rivic
'incent Roberts
)onald Roderick
oretta Rodriguez
fichael Rosenthal
iregorio Rujz
olbert Sanders
ose Sequra
)anny Seres
harles Shaw
imothy Sidie
farcelina Slazar
:obert Spears
:onald St. Claire
onny Sterling
aura Tanier
tephan Tannihil
:uisa Tapia
fichael Teague
ugene Townsend
ack Traywick
ergio Urgellas
imon Vasquez
.ron Vertiz
)avid Walker

Gregory Warner
Johnny Watson
Ron Webb
Martin Webber
Mark Weiss
Lola White
Virta White
Milburn Williams
Jimmy Williams
Donnie Wisdom
Russell Wolverton
CC Wong
Wiley "WT"

BRYAN / COLLEGE STATION (7
David Atkins
Cecil
John
Maria "Wendy" Martinez
Mr. Earl Radcliff
George Orum
Willie Sims

CORPUS CHRISTI (13)
Steve Carmona
Benjamin Clark
Leary L. Diehl
Paul D. Etie
Jose Garcia, Jr.
Kenneth Lampert
Thilden Daniel Leal
Willis Massey
Luciano Martinez, Jr.
Frank D. Mortiz
Glenn Taylor
Ricardo Rodriguez
Howard Simpson

DALLAS (11)
Anthony Burnett
Viola Gamble
Kenneth Hicks
Ed Norton
Keith Perry
Anthony Richardson
John Robinson

Esther S. George
Enrique Granado
Ronald C. Kahama
David Korach
Joe S. Link
R. D. McFarland
Debra A. Miller
L. W. Napyer
Daniel Len Ohms
Tanya D. Olney
Anthony J. Perretto
Ivan S. Selam
Delilah Dawn Stahi
Keith Tahkeal, Sr.
James Taylor
Virginia Washington
Joanna D. Yallup

WISCONSIN

KENOSHA (1)
Lance H. Turner, Jr., 36

RACINE (10)
Tim Anderson
Tiyana Campbell
Thomas E. Cobbs
Dennis Fatheree
Eric Hunchberger
LaVern Johnson
Rosalie Lunetta
Kim Mayer
Kathy Oliver
John Turner

WYOMING

CASPER (9)
Gail Boecher, 51
Steven Lockard, 46
Leslie Malloy, 48
Antonio Moore, 27
Roger Murphy, 68
Joe Paul Shollenberger, 37
Robert Skilton, 36
Paul Thompson, 69
John VanWinkle, 60

Tovar
Uncle Bert
VA
Wiley
Charlie Wilson

HOUSTON (60)
Andre Agnew
Robyn Bachand
Gloria Banks
Terrence Byrns
Connie Calhoun
Russell Castex
Ralph D Chesney
Roosevelt Churchwell
Gary Clinard
William Cowart
Jason Cummings
Lawrence Darnour
Leroy Diaz
Yvonn Drilling
Guadalupe Galindo
Javier Guerrero
Zachary Hagan
Rodney Hall
Gregory Hankins
Juan Harrelson
John Harris
Steven Hart
Andrew Hatch
Armando Hechavarria
Bonez Heflin
Lonnie Johnson
Robert Johnsted
Bobby Jones
Leonardo Lopez-Salazar
Teodoro Magana
Timothy Marshall
Reginald Thomas Mccoy
Joshua Metheny
Lola Montgomery
Edward Moone
James Moone
Ronald Nordhaus
Julian Perez
Jose Perez

Michael Pounders
Earnest Renfro
Kevin Riddick
Judy Roberts
Julio Rubio
Reynaldo Sanchez
Maria Segovia
Robert Upchurch
Jay Walls
Dennis Warren
Perry White

SAN ANTONIO (44)
Organizers have chosen not to
release names.

UTAH

SALT LAKE CITY (53)
Martin Amadour
Noe Arreola
Michael Beagley
Max Black
Teresa Lynn Blair
Thomas Boyle
Matt Castell
Lee Cheney
Clarence Cobb
Douglas Davies
Mark Dugdale
William Fechner
Richard Finley
Cesar Flores
Craig Froelich
Joan Furlong
Daniel Garcia
Bryan Hansen
James Hiatt
James Hinson
Daniel George
Joseph Hughes
Larry Hunter
Patricia Irish
Kenneth Lynn Jones
David K. Kinder
Robert Theodore Konig
Jodie L. Larsen

CHEYENNE (9)
Organizers have chosen not to
release names.

Anonymous – Even in Death

The efforts that go into collecting names for the annual memorial vigils are no substitute for a more formal system of gathering the names of people who have died while homeless, said National Coalition for the Homeless Executive Director Michael Stoops.

"We need a better system of keeping track of people who died homeless," said Stoops. But the task is just one more of the challenges of helping people who live and sometimes die in the shadows.

"When you are a homeless person, your life can be anonymous. Your death can also be anonymous. No one will know if you pass away."

Over the years, Stoops has often been called upon to identify the bodies. It's a difficult task, he said "especially when it's someone you know."

Living in Plain View, Anonymously

For homeless people and the people who work with them, it's a complicated matter. Some homeless people don't want to be named or found. Some are estranged from families or ashamed to be homeless, or in flight from justice or from abuse. Many have no identification, because it is so easily lost or stolen.

Street Sense has no formal system of keeping track of vendors and former vendors, who are not employees but independent contractors.

And their lives, like the lives of many other poor and homeless people, are often transient. Many are not reliably reachable by telephone or mail. They do not always contact the newspaper when they move on to a new job, enter a hospital or rehabilitation program, or serve time in jail.

During his March 4 visit, Andrus said he would have liked to let Street Sense know how he was doing but was it difficult while working in Virginia.

"I worked ten hours a day, six days a week. I had a cell phone and it got stolen," he said

Remembering the Deceased

National Homeless Persons' Memorial events such as the local vigil have been held nationwide every year since 1990, to remember the homeless people whose lives and deaths might otherwise go without any public recognition. The observances are co-sponsored by a number of homeless advocacy organizations including the National Coalition for the Homeless.

As I thought about all of the stories in the news, of the people who died while living in their own core of hell. I became more aware, to how blessed my life was at that very moment. Even the most horrific day I had, while living on the streets of Phoenix; I survived! I had lost everything but my life. There are people who lose their life while trying to escape homelessness.

I pushed the image of my past self out of my mind and stared at the first thing within reach. It was a well ridden, blue and quite heavy; mountain bike. It was the last thing I had put into my time capsule but the first in a procession to bring back memories of all the struggles that I endured. I overcame many obstacles in order to live the life I was now living.

Today I saw it as only a bicycle, but the person who put it in that storage saw it much differently. It was collecting dust and corroding from lack of use. The person who placed it in that storage would never have allowed such disgrace. That bike to her was the most valuable thing she could have owned. I found it difficult to believe that I was that person.

When I put that bike into storage, it was what I had needed to survive. It kept me mobile. In order to avoid police harassment I learned mobility is necessary for anyone that is homeless. I could travel to many locations at night and find things in dumpsters. My bike allowed me to be in and out of a location more quickly. When I attached my bike cart to it, I could carry many items to sell.

Without that bike, I would have gone hungry a lot more often than I did when I was homeless. I also would have found finding and selling things much more difficult.

When I first started to get back on my feet that bike was my only form of transportation to interviews, since I could not afford a bus ticket most of the time. Many times, it was my only way to get to work, after I gained employment.

I remember riding it down to the storage, and placing it in there. I never thought how time would stand still for all the possessions I had placed in that unit. I had moved on and my life has changed drastically since then; thankfully for the better.

It was time for it to help someone else. Hopefully it would be as useful for the next person. I whispered a thank you to my old blue friend as I pulled the bike out of my storage. I hoped it would bring the next person as much joy as it had for me.

There are moments that I feel the pressures and stress of my past. I still feel very broken now and then. Sometimes I stop to wonder if I will ever have any of the dreams I have held dear come true. I was forced to put my life on hold when I lost everything. I believe that time was my greatest lost. Time is something that no one can ever get back.

I had so many goals planned for myself. I hungered to be successful. The last wish I had was to become worthless and unwanted. I longed for the time and freedom to dream, and hope for granted wishes.

As I continue to dream about my future plans; I come upon a box of knick-knacks that needed to be repacked. I grab some old newspaper off of the seat of my vehicle. I notice the article in the news paper is about hurricane Katrina. I start to wrap a vase; as I try to imagine surviving that horrific night in New Orleans.

On August 29, 2005 the residents of New Orleans lost their dreams and future ideals when Katrina stormed across their city. Within a blink of an eye Mother Nature's hand took their city by force.

Katrina should have become an eye opener for everyone in our nation. Homelessness can happen to you, and is not something anyone can stop or control. How our nation handles the homelessness is in our control. I said it earlier and I will repeat this: *"If we as a nation would put half as much effort in to saving our own people as we do tot rying to save the world; we could possibly help millions."* [10]

---

10 On the next few pages are some memories from Katrina. My heart goes out to all of you who survived

Friday, November 16, 2007 Associated Press

Hurricane Katrina struck the New Orleans area early morning August 29, 2005. The storm surge breached the city's levees at multiple points, leaving 80 percent of the city submerged, tens of thousands of victims clinging to rooftops, and hundreds of thousands scattered to shelters around the country. Three weeks later, Hurricane Rita reflooded much of the area. The devastation to the Gulf Coast by these two hurricanes has been called the greatest disaster in our nation's history

Julius Nelson, 32, leader of a group called Homeless Pride that formed in the plaza, said shelters are overflowing and rental assistance is useless in a city where the storm destroyed most of the inexpensive apartments. He feared Nagin's statement meant the mayor would break up the camp.

"You've got people all over New Orleans sleeping in abandoned buildings, in abandoned cars, everywhere," Nelson said. "You don't have any affordable housing. People don't even go to the crowded shelters. They come straight here."

New Orleans has 12,000 homeless people, up from 6,300 before Katrina, according to UNITY of Greater New Orleans, a group that helps the homeless.

About 250 homeless people have erected pup-tents — the only affordable housing they say they could find since Hurricane Katrina — and created a colony of despair in a grassy plaza outside City Hall.

---

that storm.

(Press, 2007)

Some days, though, I wonder if anyone is truly free. Are you free or do you just believe a lie enforced by society? Do you get to enjoy your dreams and covet your desires? Are you blessed by granted wishes? If so then to me, at least you are truly free.

Freedom was something I had taken for granted. I could never have imagined being homeless put someone like me at risk of losing what American society takes pride in. An ominous dust covered box sat before me. A chill swept over my spine as I reached for it.

It was a box of legal papers. As I grabbed the dust covered box a law book fell off the box and onto the ground. My thoughts drifted back to 2004, the darkest year I endured when I was homeless. That year forever changed my life and how I view our justice system.

My memories focused upon the days I was in the battle of my life. I envisioned myself in the Phoenix courtroom as I began to relive the moment of being falsely accused. Ten years. A decade of my life could possibly be taken from me. The charge I faced was being in a stolen vehicle. No one wanted to believe or listen to a homeless woman's plea of innocence.

I was innocent though and wondered what I possible could have done to piss karma off. My mind filled with questions as I wondered how I could have survived so much to have my life end so abruptly. How could I have endured all the things I did in the past year to only have my life become worse? I couldn't imagine how or why my life was supposed to end so abruptly.

I replayed the past year in my head like an old movie that I had seen a hundred times. I

survived a fire. I had lost everything that I owned. My beloved cats that I treated like my children were taken. My husband abandoned me. The injuries to my hands left me with limited use of both hands for the rest of my life, and my dreams of being an artist were now put on hold. Through all of that I made myself believe life would get better.

Every incident; I made myself believe that. Now, how could I promise myself that again. I couldn't, because I suddenly felt like every hope I ever held onto was a lie. I would never imagine that someone like me could ever be falsely accused of anything.

I graduated from high school and I had some college education. I considered myself for the most part as a law abiding citizen. Even though I was being accused of theft I had never stolen anything. To me the thought of being accused of a crime you did not commit, was something only played out in a Hollywood movies. The scenario made a great script but I never imagined the thought to ever be real.

I remember trying to convince myself that the situation could be worse. I could have been fighting a life sentence or the death penalty for something I was innocent of. All of the hope I had for a brighter tomorrow was gone; I now wondered if I had enough strength left to fight.

I opened the dust covered box. I felt like I had opened a door to another dimension as I looked at the contents inside.

The box contained police reports of a crime I did not commit. I have pointed out a few facts that show my case most likely wouldn't be one of mistaken identity.

I feel the evidence was put together purposely. I am not sure what the reasoning could be. Maybe they needed to close the case or maybe they wanted me off of the streets; who knows. The excuses do not matter to me. The only thing that does matter to me is that it happened and is still happening. It will continue; as a matter of fact until someone does something.

I n opinion; everyone involved in my case, had to know or in very least come to realize, that the evidence of the crime committed clearly stated that I could not have been the perpetrator.

First off, I had been riding my bicycle. I was not in a car; I was on a bicycle. I was trying to get back home from work. I had been at work all day. At that time period in my life I had been working for a retired Mormon minister. I was part of the crew reconstructing various Mormon churches throughout Arizona.

The second conflict of interest is the race of the female in question. The eye witnesses and the police who had talked to the original suspect all collaborate and agree that a Hispanic female was the suspect in question. The police reports, the evidence, the police, the court and the state of Arizona; all eventually change the race of the woman in question to Caucasian.

Next factor is none of the eye witnesses were ever called to court. I tried every possible thing I could think of in order to have the eye witnesses there but I was never granted my wish. The eye witnesses were for the state and victims of the crime committed. I don't know about what you think, but I believe, that only an innocent person would request such a thing; or maybe someone who was crazier than I had ever been.

The police reports mention a photo lineup stating I was the person that was questioned the night of the car accident. Only the police involved in the case seen that photo lineup; none of the victims involved with the case ever saw it. In my opinion; no one's case should ever have the police become eye witnesses. The reason for my opinion is the police always are on the side of the state. Unless the officer is actually a victim; or just happen to see the crime take place they cannot truthfully claim who was at the scene of the crime. An average citizen claiming the same thing that the officers involved with my case would not ever be considered as evidence.

Finally I would like it to be known that all the evidence collected at the scene of the crime was either lost or destroyed. The state claimed that the fingerprints taken from the vehicle, the eye witnesses, and even the car could not be located for court.

I feel that my case was not one of injustice but instead a case that was unjust. In my opinion, everyone involved in my case had to see that I was without question an innocent person. I do not understand their reason for ignoring the truth.

I feel that every American in the United States should become aware of such corruption because it can happen to anyone. As a citizen, I believe our society should be appalled by cases like mine. Unjust cases in our court system, take away tax dollars that could be used for something better than putting an innocent person in prison.

I am not trying to come across as perfect. I was far from being the naive and innocent person I was months earlier when I first became homeless. By that time, I had been in and out of jail a few times. None of us are perfect, and a lot of us have skeletons in our closet. Not everyone is brave enough to open their closets like I am doing so before you stop reading and label me. I would like to point out, the crimes I have done according to society law have only hurt me and no one else.

I would also like to warn anyone who is too poor to afford their own attorney to pay close attention to cases like mine because something similar could happen to you. The following pages are copies of what was inside the box.

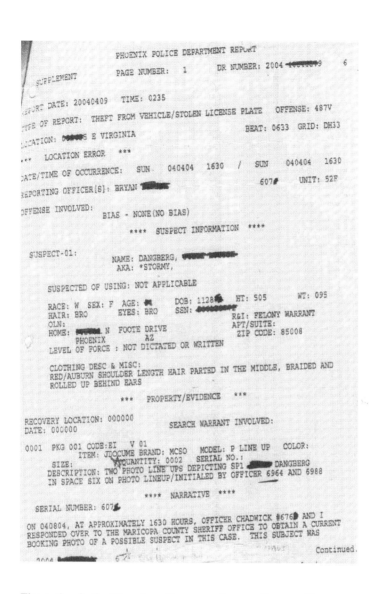

PHOENIX POLICE DEPARTMENT REPORT

SUPPLEMENT

PAGE NUMBER: 1   DR NUMBER: 2004-   9   6

REPORT DATE: 20040409   TIME: 0235

TYPE OF REPORT: THEFT FROM VEHICLE/STOLEN LICENSE PLATE   OFFENSE: 487V

LOCATION: E VIRGINIA   BEAT: 0633 GRID: DH33

*** LOCATION ERROR ***

DATE/TIME OF OCCURRENCE: SUN   040404   1630 / SUN   040404   1630

REPORTING OFFICER[S]: BRYAN   607#   UNIT: 52F

OFFENSE INVOLVED:
         BIAS - NONE (NO BIAS)

             **** SUSPECT INFORMATION ****

SUSPECT-01:
           NAME: DANGBERG,
           AKA: *STORMY,

      SUSPECTED OF USING: NOT APPLICABLE

      RACE: W SEX: F AGE: DOB: 1128   HT: 505   WT: 095
      HAIR: BRO   EYES: BRO   SSN:
      OLN: R&I: FELONY WARRANT
      HOME: N FOOTE DRIVE   APT/SUITE:
           PHOENIX   AZ   ZIP CODE: 85008
      LEVEL OF FORCE : NOT DICTATED OR WRITTEN

      CLOTHING DESC & MISC:
      RED/AUBURN SHOULDER LENGTH HAIR PARTED IN THE MIDDLE, BRAIDED AND
      ROLLED UP BEHIND EARS

             *** PROPERTY/EVIDENCE ***

RECOVERY LOCATION: 000000
DATE: 000000   SEARCH WARRANT INVOLVED:

0001 PKG 001 CODE:EI   V 01
         ITEM: JDOCUME BRAND: MCSO   MODEL: P LINE UP   COLOR:
      SIZE: QUANTITY: 0002   SERIAL NO.:
      DESCRIPTION: TWO PHOTO LINE UPS DEPICTING SP1   DANGBERG
      IN SPACE SIX ON PHOTO LINEUP/INITIALED BY OFFICER 6964 AND 6988

             **** NARRATIVE ****

SERIAL NUMBER: 607

ON 040804, AT APPROXIMATELY 1630 HOURS, OFFICER CHADWICK #676 AND I
RESPONDED OVER TO THE MARICOPA COUNTY SHERIFF OFFICE TO OBTAIN A CURRENT
BOOKING PHOTO OF A POSSIBLE SUSPECT IN THIS CASE. THIS SUBJECT WAS
                                                          Continued.
2004

Figure 1 only the Phoenix police were shown a line up. No one
else saw the lineup. At the hearing only an officer was selected as
a witness claiming I was the one in the vehicle. I asked for the
victim, witness or even the boyfriend to be brought into court but
was denied.

PHOENIX POLICE DEPARTMENT REPORT

ORIGINAL

PAGE NUMBER: 3   DR NUMBER: 2004 ~~~~~~~~

AUTO THEFT QUESTIONAIRES

	Yes	No	N/A
ARE YOU REGISTERED OWNER OF THE VEHICLE?	X		
IS THERE A LIEN ON THE VEHICLE?		X	
ARE YOU CURRENT ON THE PAYMENTS?	X		
HAVE YOU CHECKED TO SEE IF THE VEHICLE WAS REPOSSESSED BY THE LIEN HOLDER?		X	
IF YOU LOCATE THE VEHICLE, DO YOU AGREE TO NOTIFY THE POLICE DEPARTMENT IMMEDIATELY?	X		
DOES ANYONE ELSE HAVE ACCESS TO THE VEHICLE OR HAVE KEYS TO THE VEHICLE?		X	
DO YOU HAVE ANY ADDITIONAL INFORMATION OR EVIDENCE AS TO WHO HAS THE VEHICLE?		X	

PHOENIX POLICE DEPARTMENT REPORT

SUPPLEMENT   PAGE NUMBER: 1   DR NUMBER: 2004▓▓▓▓▓▓

▓▓▓RT DATE: 20040412   TIME: 0040

▓▓▓E OF REPORT: RECOVERED STOLEN VEHICLE   OFFENSE: 487V

▓▓▓SECUTION DESIRED: YES

▓▓CATION: ▓▓▓▓▓ N 19TH AVENUE   BEAT: 073▓ GRID: CD25

▓▓TE/TIME OF OCCURRENCE: SUN   040404 1630 / SUN   040404 1630

REPORTING OFFICER[S]: ▓▓▓▓▓▓ JOHNSON   699▓   UNIT: 52G
                      ▓▓▓▓ STALLMAN   696▓

PREMISES: PARKING LOT   VEHICLE

OFFENSE INVOLVED:
                BIAS - NONE(NO BIAS)

                    **** NARRATIVE ****
   SERIAL NUMBER: 6998

ON 040404 AT APPROXIMATELY 1630 HOURS, OFFICER STALLMAN #696▓ AND I
RESPONDED TO A RADIO CALL OF AN ACCIDENT AT ▓▓▓ EAST HARVARD STREET. THE
COMPLAINANT SAID THAT A WHITE 1994 NISSAN SENTRA, ARIZONA LICENSE PLATE
112▓▓, COLLIDED WITH A PARKED VEHICLE, WHICH WAS IN FRONT OF THE
APARTMENT COMPLEX AT ▓▓▓ EAST HARVARD STREET. THE COMPLAINANT ALSO
S▓▓ED THAT ONE OF THE OCCUPANTS INVOLVED SAID THAT THE NISSAN VEHICLE WAS
STOLEN.

WHEN OFFICER STALLMAN AND I ARRIVED, WE DETERMINED THAT THE WHITE NISSAN
REAR ENDED A PARKED VEHICLE, WHICH WAS ON THE SOUTH SIDE OF THE ROADWAY IN
FRONT OF THE APARTMENT COMPLEX AT ▓▓▓ EAST HARVARD STREET. BOTH VEHICLES
WERE FACING EAST.

THE WHITE NISSAN ONLY HAD FRONT END DAMAGE AND NO WINDOWS WERE BROKEN AT
THE TIME OF THIS INVESTIGATION.

TO SUM UP THE ACCIDENT INVESTIGATION, THE OWNER OF THE PARKED VEHICLE
AGREED NOT TO PURSUE ANY ACTION AGAINST THE DRIVER OF THE NISSAN SENTRA,
HOWEVER THE DRIVER OF THE NISSAN SENTRA WAS AT FAULT.

OFFICER STALLMAN SPOKE WITH THE OWNER OF THE PARKED VEHICLE AND WE DECIDED
THAT AN ACCIDENT REPORT WAS NOT NECESSARY. FOR FURTHER INFORMATION, SEE
HIS SUPPLEMENT.

AFTER THE ACCIDENT INVESTIGATION, I SPOKE WITH THE FEMALE PASSENGER, WHO
IDENTIFIED HERSELF AS KIM DANGBERG. AT THE TIME OF THIS INVESTIGATION,
KIM DID NOT HAVE ANY FORM OF IDENTIFICATION ON HER.

AFTER SPEAKING WITH OFFICER BENSON #607▓, I LEARNED THAT KIM'S TRUE
IDENTITY WAS ▓▓▓▓▓ DANGBERG. I ASKED MS. DANGBERG ABOUT THE VEHICLE AND

Figure 2 Kimberly's name isn't protected here because her last
name was changed to my last name on this document.

121

PHOENIX POLICE DEPARTMENT REPORT

NO TRAFFIC COLLISION REPORT TAKEN AT THE TIME WAS BECAUSE THE WITNESS,
I HAD SPOKEN TO, ROBERT G████, WAS APPARENTLY FRIEND'S WITH THE
OWNER OF THE VEHICLE THAT WAS STOLEN. PLEASE SEE OFFICER SHEHAN'S
SUPPLEMENT FOR FURTHER INFORMATION REGARDING THEIR CONTACT WITH THOSE
SUBJECTS.

THE TWO PHOTO LINEUPS WERE IMPOUNDED BY THIS OFFICER AT THE CENTRAL CITY
PRECINCT AS EVIDENCE.

VICTIM RECEIVED RIGHTS INFORMATION: NO   MAIL-IN SUPPLEMENT:

INVOICES: 3187██

                    END OF REPORT   DR NO: 2004██████

122

IDENTIFIED AS ████ DANGBERG, DATE OF BIRTH 1128██, WHO RESIDES AT ███ ██TH FOOTE DRIVE.

IT SHOULD BE NOTED THAT ON 040504, AT APPROXIMATELY 2045 HOURS, I RECOVERED A STOLEN VEHICLE, LICENSE PLATE 112███, AT ███ EAST HARVARD STREET. AT THAT LOCATION, I SPOKE WITH A SUBJECT IDENTIFIED AS ROBERT ██████, WHO RESIDES AT ███ EAST HARVARD STREET, APARTMENT NUMBER ██, WHO INDICATED HE HAD OBSERVED A WHITE FEMALE WHO HE DESCRIBED AS BEING APPROXIMATELY 5'5", 100 POUNDS, WITH RED AUBURNISH TYPE HAIR, WHICH WAS PARTED IN THE MIDDLE AND BRAIDED ON THE SIDES, WHICH WERE ROLLED UP BEHIND HER EARS.

WITH THAT DESCRIPTION, THE FOLLOWING DAY I WAS RIDING WITH OFFICER GILLIGAN #717 AND WERE PATROLLING THE AREA OF 25TH PLACE AND MONTE VISTA AND HAD OBSERVED A WHITE FEMALE, WHO MATCHED THE DESCRIPTION ALMOST EXACTLY. AT THAT TIME, ON 040604, AT APPROXIMATELY 1730-1800 HOURS, OFFICER GILLIGAN AND I FOUND THIS PERSON, ████ DANGBERG, HAD AN OUTSTANDING FELONY WARRANT FOR HER ARREST FOR POSSESSION OF DANGEROUS DRUGS. IN SEARCHING HER, INCIDENT TO ARREST, SHE WAS ALSO FOUND AGAIN WITH DANGEROUS DRUGS, (METHAMPHETAMINES) AS WELL AS DRUG PARAPHERNALIA. AFTER FINDING THE WARRANT AND AFTER FINDING THE NEW ITEMS OF DRUGS, SHE WAS BOOKED INTO MARICOPA COUNTY JAIL FOR THOSE CHARGES.

WITH THAT INFORMATION I SPOKE WITH AN AUTO THEFT DETECTIVE ON 040804, IN THE EARLY AFTERNOON AND DESCRIBED THE SITUATION TO HIM. HE INDICATED THAT HE HAD SPOKEN WITH OFFICER STALLMAN WHO HAD INITIALLY CONTACTED ROBERT ██████, WHO IS THE WITNESS, OUT AT 2635 HOURS AND THE DETECTIVE INDICATED FOR ME TO DO A PHOTO LINEUP WITH OFFICER STALLMAN #696█ AND OFFICER SHEHAN #6988, AS TO SEE IF IN FACT THE GIRL WHO I HAD ARRESTED WAS IN FACT THE GIRL THAT WAS PREVIOUSLY IN OR DRIVING THE STOLEN CAR ON THE PREVIOUS OCCASION.

ON 040804, AT APPROXIMATELY 1700 HOURS, I PUT TOGETHER A PHOTO LINEUP LISTING THIS ████ DANGBERG IN SPACE NUMBER █ ON A BLACK AND WHITE MARICOPA COUNTY SHERIFF'S OFFICE OFFICIAL LINE UP FORM. LATER THAT EVENING, AT APPROXIMATELY 1955 HOURS, I MET WITH OFFICER STALLMAN AND SHEHAN AND HAD THEM VIEW THE PHOTO LINEUP. I ADVISED THEM OF THE PHOTOGRAPHIC LINE UP ADVISEMENT CARD AND SHOWED FIRST OFFICER STALLMAN THE PHOTO LINE UP, TO WHICH HE IMMEDIATELY POINTED TO THE LOWER RIGHT PICTURE, WHICH IS PICTURE NUMBER █, OF ████ DANGBERG, AND STATED THAT THAT WAS THE PERSON WHO HE HAD RECOGNIZED PREVIOUSLY SITTING IN THE PASSENGER SEAT OF THE STOLEN VEHICLE. I THEN SHOWED OFFICER SHEHAN #698█, WHO ALSO VIEWED A SEPARATE BLACK AND WHITE PHOTO LINE UP AND ALSO POINTED OUT THE LOWER RIGHT CORNER PHOTOGRAPH, SPACE NUMBER █, AND ALSO INDICATED THAT THAT WAS THE GIRL WHO HE HAD SEEN IN THE STOLEN VEHICLE AT THE TIME THEY HAD CONTACTED HER.

IT SHOULD BE NOTED, HOWEVER, AT THAT TIME THEY WERE UNAWARE THAT THE VEHICLE WAS STOLEN, AS IT HAD NOT BEEN REPORTED YET.

BOTH OFFICER STALLMAN AND SHEHAN INDICATED TO ME THAT THE REASON WHY THERE

123

PHOENIX POLICE DEPARTMENT REPORT

SUPPLEMENT   PAGE NUMBER: 1   DR NUMBER: 2004 ████████

REPORT DATE: 20040409   TIME: 0007

TYPE OF REPORT: THEFT FROM VEHICLE/STOLEN LICENSE PLATE   OFFENSE: 487V

LOCATION: ███████ VIRGINIA   BEAT: 063█ GRID: DH33

.** LOCATION ERROR ***

DATE/TIME OF OCCURRENCE: SUN   040404   1630 / SUN   040404   1630

REPORTING OFFICER[S]: █████ STALLMAN   696█   UNIT: 52G
                       █████ SHEHAN   698█

OFFENSE INVOLVED:

            BIAS - NONE(NO BIAS)

                **** SUSPECT INFORMATION ****

SUSPECT-02:

              NAME ████ GABRIEL

SUSPECTED OF USING: NOT APPLICABLE

    RACE: H SEX: M AGE: ██   DOB: 05288█ HT: 508-509 WT: 150-155
    HAIR: BLK   EYES: BRO   SSN: ────
    OLN: R&I: PACE INDEX
    HOME: ██████ N 13TH PLACE   APT/SUITE:
          PHOENIX   AZ   ZIP CODE: ████
    RES.NAME: PHONE: ████████
    LEVEL OF FORCE : OFFICER PRESENCE

    EMOTIONAL CONDITIONS:CRYING   COOPERATIVE

                **** NARRATIVE ****
    SERIAL NUMBER: 696█

ON 04-04-04 AT APPROXIMATELY 1630 HOURS OFFICER SHEHAN #698█ AND I
RESPONDED TO A CALL OF A NONINJURY ACCIDENT AT ████████ VIRGINIA. UPON
ARRIVAL I CONTACTED (SP-2) GABRIEL █████. GABRIEL TOLD ME THAT HE HAD
BEEN DRIVING THE LISTED VEHICLE (PLEASE SEE ORIGINAL) AND HAD LOST
CONTROL. THE VEHICLE COLLIDED WITH A PARKED CAR THAT BELONGED TO HIS BEST
FRIEND, ROBERT ████.

WHILE I WAS TALKING WITH GABRIEL OFFICER SHEHAN WAS SPEAKING WITH A FEMALE
WHO HAD BEEN A PASSENGER IN THE CAR (PLEASE SEE HIS SUPPLEMENT).

I CHECKED THE LICENSE PLATE ON THE CAR AND IT SHOWED THAT IT WAS CURRENT
AND REGISTERED.

ROBERT AND GABRIEL WERE SPEAKING AND AGREED THAT NEITHER WISHED TO HAVE AN
ACCIDENT REPORT. THEY ALSO DISCUSSED THAT GABRIEL WOULD BE MORE THAN

2004 ████████   5   /   Continued

Figure 3 please take note of the age difference. The boyfriend is
barely above the statutory rape law. I also asked to have him
brought into court but again was refused.

IT STANDS NOW, I HAVE NO FURTHER SUSPECT INFORMATION REGARDING THE INCIDENT.

IN REGARDS TO OFFICERS SHEEHAN'S AND STALLMAN'S, I WAS UNABLE TO SPEAK WITH THEM REGARDING THE INCIDENT. I WILL ATTEMPT TO MAKE CONTACT WITH THEM LATER ON IN THE WEEK AS TO FIND OUT WHAT HAPPENED IN REGARDS TO THIS FEMALE.

AT THIS TIME, I HAVE NO FURTHER INFORMATION REGARDING THIS INCIDENT.

END OF REPORT.

JA85/A3892/6074/040604/0300/VW 0995
040604/0007/1

VICTIM RECEIVED RIGHTS INFORMATION: NO   MAIL-IN SUPPLEMENT:

INVOICES: 3185987

                         END OF REPORT   DR NO: 2004 ████████ 003

RECOVERY IMPOUND DATE: 040504

OWNER NOTIFIED: YES   DATE- 040504 TIME- 2100 BY SERIAL NO.- 607█

DISPOSITION OF VEHICLE: RELEASED TO OWNER

RECOVERY CONDITION: DRIVEABLE

NCB RECOVERY CODE: LOCAL STOLEN & LOCAL RECOVERY [IN PHX]

          ***   PROPERTY/EVIDENCE   ***

RECOVERY LOCATION: 000000
DATE: 000000   SEARCH WARRANT INVOLVED:

001 PKG 001 CODE:CI   V 01
     LAB:N ITEM: IPRINT BRAND: MODEL: LATENT   COLOR: WHI
     SIZE: QUANTITY: 0001   SERIAL NO.:
     DESCRIPTION: ONE LATENT PRINT LIFTED FROM THE OUTSIDE DRIVERS
     DOOR BY 607█

          ****   NARRATIVE ****

     SERIAL NUMBER: 607█

ON 040504 AT APPROXIMATELY 2040 HOURS, I WAS DISPATCHED TO A REPORT OF A
RECOVERED STOLEN VEHICLE AT ████ EAST HARVARD.

UPON ARRIVAL, I OBSERVED THE LISTED STOLEN VEHICLE BEING A '94 NISSAN
SENTRA, LICENSE PLATE 112██, PARKED FACING EASTBOUND ON THE SOUTH SIDE OF
THE STREET JUST EAST OF THE DRIVEWAY TO THE PARKING LOT AT ███ EAST
HARVARD.

UPON ARRIVAL, I IMMEDIATELY INSPECTED THE VEHICLE AND NOTICED THAT THE
RIGHT FRONT PASSENGER SIDE WINDOW WAS BROKEN OUT AND THERE WAS NUMEROUS
PIECES OF BROKEN GLASS BOTH INSIDE THE VEHICLE AS WELL AS OUT ON THE CURB
AS WELL AS BELOW THE PASSENGER SIDE DOOR. THIS INDICATED TO ME THAT THE
WINDOW WAS BROKEN AFTER THE VEHICLE HAD BEEN PARKED AT THIS LOCATION.

ALSO WHILE LOOKING THROUGH THE VEHICLE, I FOUND THAT ALL FOUR DOORS WERE
LOCKED; HOWEVER, THE WINDOW WAS BROKEN. I LOOKED INSIDE THE VEHICLE AND
COULD SEE THERE WERE NUMEROUS PIECES OF PERSONAL PROPERTY CLUTTERED AROUND
AND ON THE SEATS INSIDE OF THE VEHICLE AND NOTICED THAT THE GLOVE BOX
APPEARED TO HAVE BEEN FORCED OPEN OR HAD BEEN PREVIOUSLY TAPED SHUT. ALL
THE ITEMS THAT WERE PREVIOUSLY WITHIN THE GLOVE COMPARTMENT WAS STREWN
ABOUT ON THE PASSENGER SEAT AND FLOORBOARD AREA.

IT APPEARED THAT THE COLUMN WAS INTACT AND THAT NOTHING WAS TAKEN FROM THE
DASH AREA. THERE WAS NO OTHER DAMAGE TO THE VEHICLE FROM WHAT I COULD
SEE.

I ALSO LIFTED UP THE HOOD OF THE VEHICLE TO SEE IF THE BATTERY OR ANY

THEIR MOTOR PARTS HAD BEEN TAKEN AND IT APPEARED THAT THERE WEREN'T ANY PARTS MISSING.

HAVING DOCUMENTED THIS INFORMATION, I WENT BACK TO MY POLICE CAR, HAD THE INFORMATION CHANNEL OF THE PHOENIX POLICE DEPARTMENT CONTACT THE OWNER, WHO WAS ABLE TO BE CONTACTED AND ADVISED THEY WOULD BE EN ROUTE TO TAKE DISPOSITION OF THEIR VEHICLE.

I ALSO DUSTED FOR LATENT PRINTS ON THE OUTSIDE DRIVER'S SIDE DOOR AREA AS WELL AS WINDOW, DOOR FRAME, AND ROOF AREA. I LIFTED ONE LATENT PRINT FROM THE OUTSIDE DRIVER'S DOOR BELOW THE DOOR LOCK AREA. I ALSO DUSTED FOR PRINTS ON THE PASSENGER SIDE DOOR FRAME AND ROOF AREA AND WAS UNABLE TO LOCATE ANY PRINTS FROM THIS LOCATION.

UPON RETRIEVING THE PRINTS, I OBSERVED A VEHICLE PULL INTO THE PARKING LOT AND WAS LOOKING IN MY DIRECTION AS IF SOMETHING MAY HAVE BEEN WRONG OR THEY HAD INFORMATION. AFTER THESE SUBJECTS EXITED THEIR VEHICLE, I CONTACTED THEM.

THE FIRST SUBJECT I SPOKE TO IS LISTED IN THIS REPORT AS W1 ROBERT ██████. UPON SPEAKING WITH HIM, I ASKED HIM IF HE HAD OBSERVED THE VEHICLE PARKED THERE AND IF SO, FOR HOW LONG. HE INDICATED THAT HE OBSERVED THE VEHICLE PARKED THERE YESTERDAY. I INQUIRED AS TO WHETHER OR NOT HE HAD SEEN ANYBODY DRIVING IN THE VEHICLE AND HE INDICATED THAT HE DID. HE FURTHER RELATED THAT VEHICLE, BEING THE RECOVERED STOLEN VEHICLE, HAD HIT HIS PARKED VEHICLE THE DAY PRIOR ON 040404. HE WENT ON TO STATE THAT HIS VEHICLE WAS A 1990 BUICK RIVIERA, TWO DOOR, LICENSE PLATE 188██, AND HE HAD PARKED IT THERE JUST EAST OF WHERE THE RECOVERED STOLEN VEHICLE WAS ON THE DAY PRIOR AT APPROXIMATELY 1600 HOURS OR SO. HE STATED THAT HE WAS INSIDE OF HIS APARTMENT WHICH IS ● LOCATED AT THE SOUTH END OF THE COMPLEX JUST OFF OF HARVARD STREET WHEN HE WAS NOTIFIED BY HIS AUNT WHO LIVES IN APARTMENT ██ WHICH IS LOCATED DIRECTLY EAST AND THE FIRST UNIT SOUTH OF HARVARD AT ██ EAST HARVARD. HE SAID THAT HIS AUNT HAD HEARD A COLLISION OUT FRONT OF THEIR APARTMENT DIRECTLY ON HARVARD AND HAD LOOKED OUT AND OBSERVED THE RECOVERED STOLEN VEHICLE WHICH APPARENTLY CRASHED INTO HER NEPHEW'S VEHICLE, BEING ROBERT ██████ AND SHE IMMEDIATELY NOTIFIED HIM.

ROBERT INDICATED THAT HE AND HIS GIRLFRIEND, W2 PRISMA ██████, CAME FROM APARTMENT ██ AS TO CHECK OUT THE DAMAGE. ROBERT STATED THAT IMMEDIATELY UPON WALKING OUT INTO THE STREET, HE OBSERVED THE WHITE NISSAN RECOVERED STOLEN VEHICLE PROPERLY PARKED BACK ON HARVARD DIRECTLY BEHIND HIS VEHICLE AND COULD SEE THAT HIS RIGHT REAR END OF HIS VEHICLE HAD BEEN DAMAGED BY THE LEFT FRONT END OF THE RECOVERED STOLEN VEHICLE. HE INDICATED THAT THE VEHICLE HAD OBVIOUSLY PULLED UP OFF THE CURB AND IT CRASHED INTO HIS VEHICLE WHICH WAS PROPERLY PARKED ON HARVARD. HE STATED THAT HE OBSERVED A HISPANIC FEMALE WHO IDENTIFIED HERSELF TO HIM AS WELL AS HIS GIRLFRIEND AS A KIMBERLEE ██████. HE STATED THAT HE WAS EXTREMELY UPSET WITH HER AND WAS YELLING AT HER AND INQUIRING AS TO WHY IT WAS THAT SHE HAD CRASHED THE

Figure 4 please take notice of the race of the female suspect that was described to the officers. Later in the report it will have been totally changed.

SUPPLEMENT

...EN. ROBERT DID NOT MAKE ANY MENTION AS TO WHETHER OR NOT THERE WAS
...HER PEOPLE IN THE VEHICLE; HOWEVER, STATED THAT SHE WAS ATTEMPTING
...EAVE; HOWEVER, HE TOLD HER THAT SHE WAS NOT GOING TO BE ABLE TO LEAVE
... SHE HAD TO WAIT FOR THE POLICE TO COME.

...BERT INDICATED THAT HIS GIRLFRIEND, W2 PRISMA ●●●●●, WAS ALSO OUT AT
THE CURB SITE AND HAD OBSERVED THE SAME THING.

. THEN SPOKE WITH PRISMA WHO INDICATED THE FOLLOWING.

SHE STATED THAT SHE CAME OUT AND WAS ALSO YELLING AT THIS UNKNOWN
HISPANIC/WHITE FEMALE WHO IDENTIFIED HERSELF AS KIMBERLEE ●●●●●. SHE,
TOO, INDICATED THAT THIS UNKNOWN SUSPECT WAS ATTEMPTING TO LEAVE THE
ACCIDENT SCENE; HOWEVER, HAD BEEN APOLOGIZING AND INDICATED THAT SHE WOULD
PAY FOR THE DAMAGE. THEY ASKED HER IF SHE HAD ANY IDENTIFICATION AND SHE
INDICATED THAT SHE DIDN'T AND STATED TO THEM AS WELL AS WROTE IT DOWN ON A
PIECE OF PAPER THAT HER NAME WAS KIMBERLEE ●●●●● WHO DIDN'T KNOW HER
ADDRESS. SHE INDICATED AS WELL AS SHOWED ME THE PIECE OF PAPER WHICH THIS
UNKNOWN KIMBERLEE ●●●●● HAD WRITTEN ON WHICH I COULD CLEARLY SEE HAD BEEN
WRITTEN KIMBERLEE ●●●●● LISTING AN ADDRESS OF 23RD AVENUE/DUNLAP IN AN
APARTMENT OF ●●●.

BOTH ROBERT AS WELL AS PRISMA INDICATED THAT THEY DID, IN FACT, CALL THE
POLICE AND WAITED THERE AT THE CURB SITE WITH THIS UNKNOWN FEMALE UNTIL
THE POLICE ARRIVED APPROXIMATELY AN HOUR LATER. BOTH ROBERT AND PRISMA
INDICATED THE POLICE DID SHOW UP APPROXIMATELY AN HOUR LATER AND SAID
THERE WAS TWO MALE POLICE OFFICERS WHO INVESTIGATED THE INCIDENT.

PRISMA ALSO STATED THAT THIS UNKNOWN FEMALE STATED TO HER STATING, "PLEASE
DON'T CALL THE POLICE, THIS CAR IS STOLEN." PRISMA ALSO STATED THAT THIS
UNKNOWN FEMALE ALSO INDICATED THAT SHE HAD TAKEN THE VEHICLE FROM A BLACK
MALE. APPARENTLY, ROBERT AND PRISMA CALLED THE POLICE ON 040404 AT
APPROXIMATELY 1537 HOURS WHICH CAME IN ON INCIDENT ●●●●●●. THE
INFORMATION ON THAT INCIDENT INDICATED THE FOLLOWING. "SAYS PASSENGER OF
CAR THAT HIT THEIR CAR SAID THE VEHICLE WAS 487V. VEHICLE IS WHITE
CENTRAL PLATE ARIZONA 112●●. NEGATIVE NCIC/ACIC OUT OF WHITMAN,
ARIZONA."

APPARENTLY, OFFICER SHEEHAN AND OFFICER STALLMAN, HAD GONE OUT TO THIS
LOCATION AND INVESTIGATED THE INCIDENT. IT WAS DOCUMENTED IN THEIR LOG
THAT THERE WAS NO ACTION TAKEN AND THAT BOTH PARTIES INVOLVED IN THE
ACCIDENT WERE WILLING TO WORK IT OUT AMONGST THEMSELVES. THIS WAS
INFORMATION THAT WAS FOUND OUT LATER ON THAT EVENING.

ROBERT DESCRIBED THE SUBJECT INVOLVED IN THE ACCIDENT AS BEING A WHITE OR
HISPANIC FEMALE, WHO HAD HAIR THAT WAS BRAIDED AND PARTED IN THE MIDDLE
AND APPARENTLY WAS ROLLED UP ON THE SIDES BY HER EARS. HE INDICATED THAT
SHE WAS WEARING A RED OR PINK TANK TOP AND ULTIMATELY PUT ON SOME SORT OF
FLANNEL. UPON LEAVING THE ACCIDENT SCENE, WAS ALSO WEARING JEANS. HE
ALSO INDICATED THAT SHE WAS WEARING A BLACK BACKPACK THAT HAD SOME SORT OF
SECURITY TYPE BADGE AFFIXED TO IT.

Figure 5 Kimberly's last name is protected on this page. Please notice the last letter on her name because later it will be changed to my name. In this report is where the documents start to change the race of the perpetrator.

128

PRISMA INDICATED THAT SHE OBSERVED THE EXACT SAME THING AND BOTH WITNESSES INDICATED THAT THEY COULD POSITIVELY IDENTIFY THE SUBJECT IF SEEN AGAIN. THEY DESCRIBED HER AS BEING APPROXIMATELY 18 TO 20 YEARS OLD, BEING A DRUGGIE TYPE. I ASKED WHAT THEY MEANT BY THAT AND THEY INDICATED THAT SHE LOOKED LIKE SHE WAS TWIKING ON SOME SORT OF DRUGS. THEY STATED THAT SHE WAS VERY NERVOUS THROUGHOUT THE ENTIRE INCIDENT AND WANTED ONLY TO LEAVE. THEY INDICATED THAT SHE TOLD THEM THAT SHE WOULD RETURN WITH THE MONEY TO PAY FOR THE DAMAGE THAT SHE HAD DONE TO THEIR BUICK UPON RUNNING UP THE CURB AND STRIKING INTO THE REAR END OF IT.

THEY DESCRIBED HER AS BEING APPROXIMATELY 100-115 POUNDS, AND APPROXIMATELY 5'5" WITH BROWN EYES AND REDDISH BROWN TYPE HAIR. STATED THAT SHE WAS VERY SKINNY AND LOOKED LIKE SHE WAS ON DRUGS. ROBERT STATED THAT THE OFFICERS SPOKE TO HER AND THAT SHE ULTIMATELY WALKED AWAY FROM THE ACCIDENT SITE. IT IS UNKNOWN AT THIS TIME, WHAT, IN FACT, THE OFFICERS DID DO AT THAT TIME DUE TO THE FACT THAT I WAS UNABLE TO SPEAK TO EITHER OF THEM, AS THEY WERE OFF THE REMAINDER OF THE WEEK.

WHILE SPEAKING WITH BOTH ROBERT AND PRISMA, THE VICTIM WHO IS IDENTIFIED AS PAMELA ███████, DATE OF BIRTH 0610██, ARRIVED ALONG WITH HER BOYFRIEND. SHE INDICATED THAT THERE WAS NOTHING TAKEN AS FAR AS THEY COULD TELL FROM THE INSIDE OF THE VEHICLE WITH THE EXCEPTION OF THEIR CELL PHONE; HOWEVER, THEY DID NOT PROVIDE ANY FURTHER INFORMATION REGARDING THE PHONE AND I NEGLECTED TO GET THAT INFORMATION.

PAMELA WAS ABLE TO START THE VEHICLE AND HER BOYFRIEND ULTIMATELY DROVE IT AWAY FROM THE AREA. I MENTIONED TO THEM BEFORE THEY LEFT IF THEY KNEW ANYBODY BY THE NAME OF KIMBERLEE ██████ AND THEY INDICATED THAT THEY DIDN'T. I ASKED THEM IF THEY WERE WILLING TO PRESS CHARGES IF, IN FACT, A SUSPECT WERE TO BE APPREHENDED AND THEY INDICATED THAT THEY WOULD.

THEY BRIEFLY DESCRIBED TO ME THE CIRCUMSTANCES REGARDING THE VEHICLE BEING STOLEN IN THE FIRST PLACE. THEY STATED THEY WERE AT THE IHOP AT 19TH AVENUE AND GLENDALE THE DAY PRIOR. THEY STATED THAT THEY WERE ONLY THERE FOR APPROXIMATELY 20 TO 25 MINUTES. WHEN THEY CAME OUT, THEIR VEHICLE HAD BEEN STOLEN.

AT THAT TIME, THE VICTIM TOOK DISPOSITION OF THEIR VEHICLE. I BRIEFLY SPOKE WITH BOTH ROBERT AND PRISMA A LITTLE MORE WHO INDICATED THAT IF, IN FACT, THEY OBSERVED THIS FEMALE AGAIN, THEY WOULD SURELY, IN FACT, CALL THE POLICE.

BOTH WITNESSES INDICATED THAT THEY COULD POSITIVELY IDENTIFY THIS SUBJECT IF SEEN AGAIN.

LATER ON BACK AT THE STATION, I ATTEMPTED TO DO FOLLOW UP BY LOOKING UP THE NAME KIMBERLEE ██████ ON THE COMPUTER; HOWEVER, RECEIVED ONLY THREE POSSIBLE MATCHES, NONE LISTING ANY TYPE OF APARTMENT NEAR 23RD AVENUE AND DUNLAP. NO FURTHER INFORMATION AS TO LINK THEM TO THIS CRIME.

Figure 6 the race of female is completely changed in this report.

129

WITNESS -02:   NAME: ███████ PRISMA

RACE: H SEX: F AGE: █   DOB: 04298█   HT: 409   WT: 130
HAIR: BRO   EYES: BRO   SSN: 000000000

CLOTHING DESC & MISC:
GIRLFRIEND TO W1/ALSO OBSERVED SUSPECT
HOME: █████E HARVARD STREET   APT/SUITE: █
        PHOENIX   AZ   ZIP CODE: ████
RES NAME: PHONE: ████
CAN ID SUSPECT(S): YES   SUSPECT(S): SP1
WILL TESTIFY: YES   MISC.

**** RECOVERED VEHICLE ****

VEHICLE NUMBER: 01   INVOLVED PERSON: V-01   IS NOT ON THIS REPORT

LAST KNOWN DIRECTION OF TRAVEL: EASTBOUND

VEHICLE   YEAR: 94   MAKE: NISS   MODEL: SENTRA   STYLE: 4D
    VIN: █████4RC908270   OAN:
    VALUE: $1500   CONDITION: RUNNING
    COLOR: TOP/SOLID-WHI

    LICENSE PLATE: 112███   STATE: AZ   TYPE: PC YEAR: 04

FEATURES: DAMAGE TO FRONT

FURTHER DESC.: BROKEN PASSENGER SIDE WINDOW

METHOD USED TO STEAL: NOT DICTATED

OWNER NAME: UNKNOWN -- V 01   REGISTERED TO OWNER: YES

WRECKER/TOW CO. PREFERRED: LIST

FOJ INFORMATION: ORI#:   OCA#: 2004█████

        NIC#: V016████   FAV: APP:

        **** RECOVERY/IMPOUND INFORMATION ****

RECOVERY IMPOUND GRID: RE:█

RECOVERY/IMPOUND LOCATION: ████ E HARVARD STREET
                           PHOENIX   AZ

Continued

PHOENIX POLICE DEPARTMENT REPORT

PAGE NUMBER: 1   DR NUMBER: 2004-■■■ 8

SUPPLEMENT

REPORT DATE: 20040412   TIME: 1520   OFFENSE: 487V

TYPE OF REPORT: RECOVERED STOLEN VEHICLE

BEAT: 0732 GRID: CD25

LOCATION: ■■■ N 19TH AVENUE

DATE/TIME OF OCCURRENCE: SUN   040404   1630   /   SUN   040404   1630

592■   UNIT: P58

REPORTING OFFICER(S): ■■■ ROBINSON

OFFENSE INVOLVED:
                  BIAS - NONE(NO BIAS)

REPORT STATUS AT PRESENT: PENDING

                  **** NARRATIVE ****

SERIAL NUMBER: 592■

I WAS ASSIGNED THE INVESTIGATION OF THIS STOLEN/RECOVERED VEHICLE REPORT.
AFTER REVIEWING THE CASE, I TALKED TO OFFICER BENSON, THE ONE WHO
RECOVERED THE VEHICLE. [SEE HIS SUPPLEMENT FOR HIS INFORMATION].

...ERMINED THAT SP1 WAS IN THE STOLEN VEHICLE AND KNEW IT WAS
...AT THE ACCIDENT IT WAS STOLEN. A FILESTOP WILL
... UNLAWFUL USE.

131

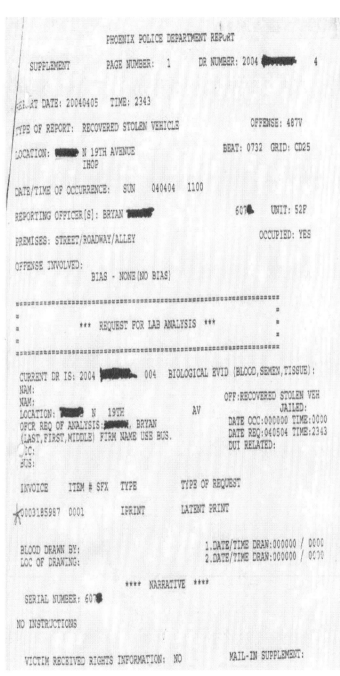

PHOENIX POLICE DEPARTMENT REPORT

SUPPLEMENT   PAGE NUMBER: 1   DR NUMBER: 2004 ████████   4

START DATE: 20040405   TIME: 2343

TYPE OF REPORT: RECOVERED STOLEN VEHICLE   OFFENSE: 487V

LOCATION: ████ N 19TH AVENUE   BEAT: 0732 GRID: CD25
          IHOP

DATE/TIME OF OCCURRENCE: SUN   040404   1100

REPORTING OFFICER[S]: BRYAN ████   607█   UNIT: 52P

PREMISES: STREET/ROADWAY/ALLEY   OCCUPIED: YES

OFFENSE INVOLVED:
            BIAS - NONE[NO BIAS]

===
 =   =
 =   *** REQUEST FOR LAB ANALYSIS ***   =
 =   =
===

CURRENT DR IS: 2004 ████ 004 BIOLOGICAL EVID [BLOOD,SEMEN,TISSUE]:
NAM:
NAM: OFF:RECOVERED STOLEN VEH
LOCATION: ████ N 19TH   AV   JAILED:
OFCR REQ OF ANALYSIS:████, BRYAN   DATE OCC:000000 TIME:0000
[LAST,FIRST,MIDDLE] FIRM NAME USE BUS. DATE REQ:040504 TIME:2343
OC: DUI RELATED:
BUS:

INVOICE   ITEM # SFX TYPE   TYPE OF REQUEST

0003195987 0001   IPRINT   LATENT PRINT

BLOOD DRAWN BY: 1.DATE/TIME DRAW:000000 / 0000
LOC OF DRAWING: 2.DATE/TIME DRAW:000000 / 0000

                **** NARRATIVE ****

SERIAL NUMBER: 607█

NO INSTRUCTIONS

VICTIM RECEIVED RIGHTS INFORMATION: NO   MAIL-IN SUPPLEMENT:

Figure 7 at court the fingerprints were claimed as lost

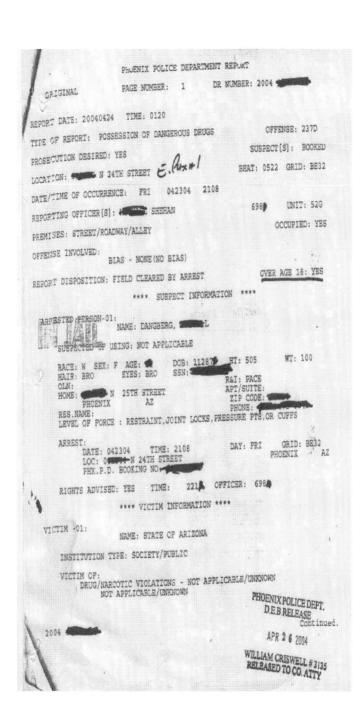

PHOENIX POLICE DEPARTMENT REPORT

ORIGINAL

PAGE NUMBER: 1   DR NUMBER: 2004 ████████

REPORT DATE: 20040424   TIME: 0120

TYPE OF REPORT: POSSESSION OF DANGEROUS DRUGS

PROSECUTION DESIRED: YES

LOCATION: ████ N 24TH STREET E. Rx#1

DATE/TIME OF OCCURRENCE: FRI   042304   2108

REPORTING OFFICER(S): ██████ SHERAN

PREMISES: STREET/ROADWAY/ALLEY

OFFENSE INVOLVED:
                  BIAS - NONE (NO BIAS)

REPORT DISPOSITION: FIELD CLEARED BY ARREST

OFFENSE: 237D

SUSPECT(S): BOOKED

BEAT: 0522 GRID: BE32

698█   UNIT: 52G

OCCUPIED: YES

OVER AGE 18: YES

**** SUSPECT INFORMATION ****

ARRESTED PERSON-01:
                      NAME: DANGBERG, ██████L
          SUSPECTED OF USING: NOT APPLICABLE

RACE: W SEX: F AGE: ██   DOB: 1128██ HT: 505   WT: 100
HAIR: BRO   EYES: BRO   SSN:██████
OLN: R&I: PACE
HOME: ████ N 25TH STREET   APT/SUITE:
      PHOENIX   AZ   ZIP CODE:██████
                                         PHONE: ██████
RES.NAME:
LEVEL OF FORCE : RESTRAINT,JOINT LOCKS,PRESSURE PTS,OR CUFFS

ARREST:
        DATE: 042304   TIME: 2108   DAY: FRI   GRID: BE32
        LOC: 0████ N 24TH STREET   PHOENIX   AZ
        PHX.P.D. BOOKING NO ████████

RIGHTS ADVISED: YES   TIME: 221█ OFFICER: 698█

**** VICTIM INFORMATION ****

VICTIM -01:
                 NAME: STATE OF ARIZONA

INSTITUTION TYPE: SOCIETY/PUBLIC

VICTIM OF:
         DRUG/NARCOTIC VIOLATIONS - NOT APPLICABLE/UNKNOWN
         NOT APPLICABLE/UNKNOWN

PHOENIX POLICE DEPT.
D.E.B RELEASE
Continued.

2004 ████

APR 2 6 2004

WILLIAM CRISWELL #3135
RELEASED TO CO. ATTY

133

PHOENIX POLICE DEPARTMENT REPORT

ORIGINAL   PAGE NUMBER: 1   DR NUMBER: 2004 ██████

REPORT DATE: 20040404   TIME: 1539

TYPE OF REPORT: STOLEN VEHICLE   OFFENSE: 487V

PROSECUTION DESIRED: YES

LOCATION: ████ N 19TH AVENUE *E.Phxb'*   BEAT: 0732 GRID: CD25
          IHOP

DATE/TIME OF OCCURRENCE: SUN   040404 1100 /   1200

REPORTING OFFICER[S]: ████ CLEMONS   A404█   UNIT: CALL

PREMISES: PARKING LOT   RESTAURANT

OFFENSE INVOLVED:
              BIAS - NONE(NO BIAS)

                **** VICTIM INFORMATION ****

  VICTIM -01:
              NAME: ██████, PAMELA

    RACE: W SEX: F AGE: 25   DOB: 0610██ HT: 000   WT: 000

    VICTIM OF:
            MOTOR VEHICLE THEFT - COMPLETED
      HOME: APT/SUITE:
                                         ZIP CODE
      RES.NAME: PHONE: ███ ████
      WORK: APT/SUITE:
      BUS.NAME: PHONE: EXT.
      OCCUPATION: █████
      WORK HOURS: 0700 - 1500   DAYS OFF: SS

    VICTIM REQUESTS NOTIFICATION

                **** STOLEN VEHICLE ****

  VEHICLE NUMBER: 01   INVOLVED PERSON: V-01 ████R PAMELA

  VEHICLE   YEAR: 94   MAKE: NISS   MODEL: SENTRA   STYLE: 4D
      VIN: 1N4EB31P4RC80███   OAN:
      VALUE: $2000   CONDITION: RUNNING
      COLOR: TOP/SOLID-WHI

    LICENSE PLATE: 112███   STATE: AZ   TYPE: PC   YEAR: 04

  METHOD USED TO STEAL: UNKNOWN

  OWNER NAME: UNKNOWN -- 00
                                        PHOENIX POLICE DEPT.: YES
                                        D.E.B RELEASE
  2004 ██████   Continued.
                                        APR 2 6 2004

                                        WILLIAM CRISWELL #3135
                                        RELEASED TO CO. ATTY

NON-DANGEROUS OFFENSES

CLASS	FIRST OFFENSE			ONE HISTORICAL PRIOR			TWO HISTORICAL PRIORS		
	MIN	P	MAX	MIN	P	MAX	MIN	P	MAX
2	(3)*4	5	10 (12.5)†	(4.5)*6	9.25	18.5 (23.25)†	(10.5)*14	15.75	28 (35)†
3	(2)*2.5	3.5	7 (8.75)†	(3.5)*4.5	6.5	13 (16.25)†	(7.5)*10	11.25	20 (25)†
4	(1)*1.5	2.5	3 (3.75)†	(2.25)*3	4.5	6 (7.5)†	(6)*8	10	12 (15)†
5	(.5)*.75	1.5	2 (2.5)†	(1)*1.5	2.25	3 (3.75)†	(3)*4	5	6 (7.5)†
6	(.33)*.5	1	1.5 (2)†	(.75)*1	1.75	2.25 (2.75)†	(2.25)*3	3.75	4.5 (5.75)†

Probation eligible, except for single drug offenses involving manufacture or in which the amount exceeds the statutory threshold. Convictions for first offense sexual assault: minimum of 5.25 years, presumptive of 7 years and a maximum of 14 years with no early release unless the sentence is commuted.

NON-DANGEROUS OFFENSES - MULTIPLE OFFENSES - (§ 13-702.02)

CLASS	SECOND OFFENSE			SUBSEQUENT OFFENSES		
	MIN	P	MAX	MIN	P	MAX
2	(3)*4	5	10 (12.5)†	(4.5)*6	9.25	18.5 (23.25)†
3	(2)*2.5	3.5	7 (8.75)†	(3.5)*4.5	6.5	13 (16.25)†
4	(1)*1.5	2.5	3 (3.75)†	(2.25)*3	4.5	6 (7.5)†
5	(.5)*.75	1.5	2 (2.5)†	(1)*1.5	2.25	3 (3.75)†
6	(.33)*.5	1	1.5 (2)†	(.75)*1	1.75	2.25 (2.75)†

DANGEROUS OFFENSES

CLASS	FIRST OFFENSE			ONE HISTORICAL DANGEROUS PRIOR			TWO HISTORICAL DANGEROUS PRIORS		
	MIN	P	MAX	MIN	P	MAX	MIN	P	MAX
2	7	10.5	21	14	15.75	28	21	28	35
3	5	7.5	15	10	11.25	20	15	20	25
4	4	6	8	8	10	12	12	14	16
5	2	3	4	4	5	6	6	7	8
6	1.5	2.25	3	3	3.75	4.5	4.5	5.25	6

DANGEROUS OFFENSES - MULTIPLE OFFENSES - (§ 13-702.02)

CLASS	SECOND DANGEROUS OFFENSE		SUBSEQUENT DANGEROUS OFFENSES	
	MIN/P	MAX	MIN/P	MAX
2	10.5	21 (26.25)†	15.75	28 (35)†
3	7.5	15 (18.75)†	11.25	20 (25)†
4	6	8 (10)†	10	12 (15)†
5	3	4 (5)†	5	6 (7.5)†
6	2.25	3 (3.75)†	3.75	4.5 (5.75)†

* Approximate 25% reduction: 2 or more substantial mitigating factors. A.R.S. §13-702.01
† Approximate 25% increase: 2 or more substantial aggravating factors. A.R.S. §13-702.01

A defendant may earn release credits of one day for every six days served. Commutation is possible.

A person convicted of a violent crime as defined in A.R.S. §13-604.04 committed while the person is under the influence of marijuana, a dangerous drug or a narcotic drug is not eligible for release or probation until the entire sentence has been served.

The court shall increase by up to two years the maximum sentence for any felony causing physical injury committed against a pregnant victim known by the person to be pregnant.

(3)

While some cities and states have taken positive steps, there are still many parts of the United States that continue to dehumanize homeless persons by creating and enforcing laws that criminalize their homeless status. These laws contain restrictions on sitting, sleeping, storing property, or asking for money in public spaces. Laws that criminalize the homeless encourage the belief that homeless persons are not human, are unworthy of respect, and attacks against the homeless will go unnoticed.

(Lee, 2009)

American Girl's Homeless Doll

At the NY Post, <u>Andrea Peyser</u>, who calls the American Girls line, "middle American Crack," wrote of the doll: "For $95 -- more than your average homeless person would dream of spending on a rather mediocre baby substitute -- Gwen Thompson can be yours. A mixed message if ever there was one." One homeless woman in a shelter Kauffman visited said Gwen touched her heart when she saw the doll in its box. The women praised the doll, Kauffman reports, until they learned Gwen isn't a fundraising device for the homeless. "I don't even see why you would make a homeless doll, anyway," one woman said to Kauffman, unless it was being used to raise money to help charities aiding the homeless. There's a fine line

between advocacies and, well, poor taste. The ever-popular American Girls brand has released a controversial new doll named "Gwen," a character who's actually homeless.

America, we should be appalled by this propaganda! Doll's target children and stimulatat reason.

Figure 8 below are what a few of you are saying America. I put some of the worst and best comments in this book. All of them are unanimous.

⋆   *It's the American way. Make money out of anything.*

⋆   *Leave it to Mattel to capitalize on one of the social ills in our society. Leave no stone unturned in order to make a buck. Mattel isn't even do*

⋆   *donating any proceeds from the sales of this doll to homeless shelters or agencies that would assist homeless people, although they do donate to charities in general -- just not with this particular doll. Seems stupid and illogical. Mattel ruined the American Girls dolls brand.*

⋆   *This is great. You don't have to worry about buying the doll a lot of accessories or even a house. She can live in the box she comes in.*

⋆   *What would happen if Mattel produced a doll with AIDS and didn't donate the proceeds to an AIDS charity?*

⋆   *Girl doll is homeless. She is homeless in her story because her dad leaves her and Im sorry, maybe I'm misunderstanding. Gwen, the American her mom and the mom is unable to financially support them -- and they end up homeless. How does that not represent what happens to people? It is shameful that Mattel would create such a doll and then not donate the proceeds to a homeless shelter or agency that benefits homeless people. The doll costs $95 dollars. Who can afford that? Not homeless people. Why create a homeless doll at all? What statement was Mattel trying to make? Just that crap happens and sometimes people become homeless...oh well? Maybe it would have been a "teaching moment" had Mattel thought to donate the proceeds to benefit people that really need support and assistance to get back on their feet.*

★ *Checked the website, and from what I'm seeing, the doll isn't really designed to represent the homeless, so much as being simply a representation of a character in a book.*

★ *I believe there's a car sold separately that she lives in...*
(Peyser)

Chapter Five

ENDURANCE

As I pick up the musty pages from their time capsule; I hear a detention officers voice bellow in my head.

"Lock down," screams a D.O. "Ladies, Lock down!"

A chaotic world of turmoil and demands face me as I step into the overpopulated room called a cell. Lock down, I realized quickly that it translates to get own your bunks and to stay put.

I am directed to one of the metal trays; stacked about three high and four in a row; dividing the room in half. There are six of these four row bunks on each side of the room.

"Here is your home," said a middle-age, blonde with a toothless smile; as she pointed to a bed with the number ninety-two on it.

"Thanks," I said as I climbed up to the third metal tray thinking to myself that this will not be home for me. I would make sure of that.

I would do everything in my power to win this battle of innocence.

I tuned out the chaos below as I close my eyes and drifted into a restless sleep. I hear someone tapping on my metal frame. I sat up and looked down.

"Time for court," said a rather young red head woman below me."It is midnight; time for court."

I looked around the room and saw women scurrying like little mice in a field. Some; were getting clean prison camp attire. A few inmates were getting razors by trading their mug shot I.D.

Everyone was in a hustle and bustle; it seemed, except for me. I didn't see any reason to be in a hurry to be shackled and it seemed pointless to play pretend dress up for court. No matter what I did, the judge would not look at me any different. While in handcuffs and prison attire; I would be seen only as an inmate. I laid back down and listened carefully for my name to be called. Only when it was time to be lined up for shackles and handcuffs would I move.

At two in the morning the inmates line up in a single file line down a hall that links all the cells together. We are shackled and handcuffed together in groups of two and three. Then we were herded like cattle onto a bus, in order to be transferred to court.

After being herded onto the bus us inmates ride silently to the courthouse. At the courthouse the detention officer takes our handcuffs off but the shackles remain around our ankles.

I look around and notice the women; who have been through this countless times tucking their pants under the shackle cuffs. Not very long, I understood why and did the same. It was a little late for me to follow suit; the thick metal cuffs already done their damage to my legs. Visible blistering sores were painfully noticeable by the time I copied the other women.

We are then shuffled from one cell to another for no other reason it seems other than to amuse our captors. Nearly 4:00 AM we are handed a lunch sack assisting of fruit, crackers, and three sandwiches. It is a typical brown bag lunch sack except juice is given in place of milk. Usually that brown bag lunch is suppose to last all day. At court no food is allowed so that means we would only be eating what we wanted or could until we would be shuffled off to court.

There are about eight inmates in a 5 by 7 foot cell. Everyone holds the same dismal expression of despair and hope. At 8:30 AM the inmates are once again shuffled to a different cell and wait see the judge.

Court for an inmate is an all day affair. At about 5:00 PM, I'm again shuffled onto a bus to go back to jail to be released. It was a victorious moment for me, but a daunting one as well. The term freedom, was only temporary for me unless I could win my case.

While I was in jail I was given the news that I was pregnant. The news made me more worried about the pending trial. My baby became the strength to fight for justice. The false charges no longer affected just me but my child as well.

Imagine, for one moment, having the responsibility of taking care of a child while being homeless. Visualize, someone so innocent, so small; leaning on you for support, and looking up to you for help. I don't think anyone could possibly imagine the depressing feeling of failure a homeless mother or father must be burdened with.

Many people I believe feel that the individual and not circumstances cause homelessness. Some people might even go as far to say that a person brought being homelessness upon themselves. Even if the adult had something to do with their demise, what did the child do? What choice did a child have?

If the solution, take the child away enters your mind, again I ask you; what did the child do? Why should children have the only foundation they cling to be ripped away? I could never see how

anyone could conclude that families would be better apart.[11]

11 The next few pages contain an article about homeless children in
America.

We shouldn't have homeless children in America

By David A. Love | *Juneau Empire*

One million schoolchildren are homeless in America. That's an intolerable number, and it's likely to rise unless we do something about it.

For homeless school-age children - with precarious living arrangements and the daily struggles to find food and shelter - attending school is an uphill battle. At least one-fifth do not attend school at all. Often, there is no transportation from shelters to school.

And for those homeless students who do attend, they have more academic problems, are suspended twice as often, and are more likely to repeat a grade. Their math and reading scores are 16 percent lower, and only one in four graduates from high school.

We are punishing these school-age kids for the sins of our economic and social policies.

Starting with President Reagan, the federal government has made one cut after another in the social safety net. President Clinton overturned our welfare policies. And Presidents Bush father and son both were unfriendly to the poor.

Today's hard times have only made things worse. The recession, brought on by reckless Wall Street gambling, has brought on an epidemic of foreclosures and layoffs.

With foreclosures and layoffs particularly high in communities of color, the black and Latino middle class are joining the burgeoning ranks of the homeless. In fact, children of color now constitute a majority of the homeless.

In 1996, 66 percent of homeless parents with children under 18 were white, 15 percent were black, 14 percent Hispanic, 1 percent American Indian and 4 percent other. But in 2006, 38 percent of homeless parents were white, 47 percent were black, 13 percent were Hispanic, 2 percent were American Indian, with 1

*percent other. (All statistics in this article come from the National
Center on Family Homelessness.)*

The effects of homelessness on children are crippling.

*Children who are homeless are in bad health twice as often
as other children, and four times as often as children with a family
annual income of more than $35,000. They are four times as likely to
have asthma, and they go hungry twice as often as other children.*

*Homeless children have delayed development at a rate four
times the national average. More than one-fifth of homeless children
between 3 and 6 years have emotional problems that require
professional attention.*

*We can eliminate childhood homelessness if we have the
will.*

*The federal government should invest $10 billion over two
years to building 100,000 rental homes, funding 400,000 new
housing vouchers for $3.6 billion, and investing $3 billion for child
care vouchers for homeless children.*

*Meanwhile, states and localities can make homelessness a
priority, place families into permanent housing rather than motels
and prevent the removal of children into foster care solely because of
homelessness.*

*Critics of "big government" will say that America can't
afford such an expense in a recession, that we simply don't have the
money. But we have the money, somehow, to bail out Wall Street to
the tune of trillions of dollars. We have the money, somehow, to wage
two wars that are draining trillions more from our Treasury.*

*Critics of social spending on homelessness also believe
that poverty is someone else's problem, the result of laziness,
immorality or bad life choices. But the United States has never had
enough good-paying jobs for all who need them. Besides, what
choice does a child have about her family's income level?*

*In our Great Recession, many people are a paycheck, a
mortgage payment or a hospital bill away from homelessness, a fate*

that is especially cruel to their children. It should not be too much to guarantee our nation's kids a roof over their heads.

• David A. Love is a writer for Progressive Media Project, a source of liberal commentary on domestic and international issues; it is affiliated with The Progressive magazine.

(Lowe)

I immediately did everything I could to make sure I would have a healthy child. I was living with her father at the time, which made it easier to stay away from the streets and drugs that had been afflicting my life since I had landed on them. I learned that I was going to have a girl and I named her Usenda Storm. I was due to have her on February 14th, Valentine's Day.

Her Father's name is Greg. He is a tall, older gentleman with grey to green eyes and graying hair. He is much older than me. He is close to twenty years older as a matter of fact.

I met him while I was living in a tent behind a drug dealer's house. I was campsite number four. I had a small pup tent that I was living in. He would come to the house on a regular basis before heading off to work at the Home Depot.

When I first met him he was always so kind and generous; not to just me but almost everyone at that house. He invited everyone to a barbeque one evening and from there we quickly became friends.

Since that night he has been in and out of my life. He can be mean as much as he can be kind. It all depends on his mood. Over the years we have been lovers, friends and enemies. Our relationship has always been a roller coaster of drama.. We have a relationship that can change from one day to the next.

A few weeks after I was released from jail; he was booked into jail on drug charges; leaving me alone with not only my problems but his as well. I suddenly inherited a whole apartment that needed to be packed, a pending court battle and a decision of what would happen to our daughter.

It became clear, that a lawyer was out of the picture for Usenda and me. Without funds, I was forced to rely on a public defender. Maybe some people who are public defenders act as a real paid lawyer. The lawyer I had, I felt, as though she acted like she was not getting paid at all for my case . The small amount of effort that she put towards my case, came across to me, that I was not worth fighting for.

I did my own footwork by spending almost every free moment at the law library. I had a notebook full of notes and could recite most of the A.R.S. codes by heart the first time that I had met with her.

Unfortunately, for me, I was in a losing battle. It was not the fact that the Phoenix police had overwhelming evidence but the fact that no one cared about a homeless woman enough to fight for her. I was unimportant to the general society. My attorney even at one time; pointed out the idea that I shouldn't be worried about jail time due to I had no ties to the outside world.

My life felt so unraveled. I would spend countless hours pacing, and crying, as my mind would replay the turmoil of my life. I knew I was sinking further into a depression but I had no clue how to control my emotions.

I felt like I was in an eye of a storm because occasionally I found peace. I treasured those days because I knew something would arise, some problem, I would have to deal with. My whole life was surrounded by turmoil. I knew that a peaceful moment was only the quiet before the storm. I could never imagine the worse due to whatever I faced was always much greater than I could believe.

I remember the day I noticed I was losing touch with reality. It was a day that I felt emotionally and physically disconnected to myself. I no longer knew who I was as a person. Emotions of sadness filled my soul from not feeling that connection.

Sitting in front of a mirror one day, I noticed I no longer felt a connection to the image that stared back at me. I believe we all have a feeling of self when staring at our reflection. Somehow, I had lost that. I knew the image staring back at me was myself, but felt no emotional connection.

Kneeling in front of that mirror, tears filled my eyes as I stared carefully at the stranger looking back at me. Fear, pain, and anger overwhelmed me. I felt so empty and hollow to the point I wanted to die. Anger surged through every nerve of my body towards everyone who pushed me to that point of insanity. Fear of going further insane rushed over me.

"Where are you?" I screamed at the reflection as I pounded on the mirror,

"Come back! Please… come back," I sobbed at the reflection distraughtly.

I wanted so desperately to feel that correlation of self again. I felt so fragmented and shattered.   I crumpled into a ball sobbing uncontrollably as my thoughts returned to Joe. I wondered if this was how he felt. Did he ever feel as disconnected as me? Could one of my greatest fears be coming true? Was I slowly becoming lost to everyone; including myself? If so, could I find my way back to reality, and how?

Days and nights slowly became a blur as I began to lose focus with reality. I sank into my own world. There were days where I could not tell if I was dreaming or living through another ordeal.

My mind wandered; in and out of the realm of reality. Countless emotions followed every thought. Some things; I have learned are indescribable. I know now that the unimaginable can be real and reality can feel inconceivable.

I developed a twisted habit during those darkest days in the core. In order to know if I was awake or dreaming I began to cut myself. Living under the veil of insanity; it was easier to focus on physical pain than mental anguish. I knew what I was experiencing at that moment in time was indeed real if I could feel the physical pain.

Now that I am no longer a fragmented person I can relate to your reason to not understanding my judgment during that time. I said it earlier about Joe, and now I will remind you of the only explanation I know, *"Sometimes I mourn for the hidden truth that lies behind the agony of insanity."*

I warn everyone never to wish for that truth to much because you don't really want to know the agony of insanity. It is not a good place to be. Take that advice from someone who knows firsthand.

I thought about the life growing inside me as I contemplated thoughts of suicide. I faced so many difficulties that I was uncertain about. I could not take care of myself. How could I possibly be able to give my child any future that I thought she deserved? Unless I chose adoption, I knew no one in society would support any decision I made.

The whole concept of me being pregnant felt ironic. Almost every day I hoped and prayed for death, but yet another life was growing inside of me. Her birthday was a paradoxical itself. She was surrounded by turmoil and hate but due to be born on the day of love. Neither of our worlds made any sense, in my opinion.

I was about four months along and I already knew her name. I desperately wanted to be making a home for her. I again longed for normalcy in my life. I would see other women planning and buying things for their child, in order to be prepared for their home coming, after being born. I wanted the same for Usenda and me. Only in my dreams that realm of reality existed.

My love for her grew as much as my heart ached for her. She had such a bleak future and she was not even born yet. I knew the chances of me ever holding her were slim to none. I knew her father's family desperately wanted to raise her. At that time in my life that idea was not an option for me because I felt I could trust their intentions. I also felt Usenda deserved love and I believed she would not really feel that from her father because he acted as though wanted nothing to do with her after conception.

She was not planned for but I felt, at that time in my life that only her father considered her a mistake. I felt that her father had other intentions for wanting her. I believed, sadly, she was becoming a pawn, in a world she did not know.

As a child, I was taught that people get what they deserve in this world. Today, I question such idiocy. I could not comprehend how Usenda or I deserved any of the chaos and turmoil we faced.

Having a child, I have always known to be a happy time in one's life. I thought I would have the same joy and excitement as most women. I would never have imagined the notion of such feelings being destroyed.

I knew I faced jail time and wondered what kind of life she could have without me in it. The idea of reuniting with her entered my mind. Would I be able to raise my own child? If I ever was allowed, I wondered if I was capable. How much time would pass, before I could be allowed to show her my love? Would she want to have me in her life? Or would she be corrupted by the lies I knew she would be told about me?

I started to think about the options I had left for her. The option of raising my daughter had been taken away but I knew there were other options for her. I felt that if I really did love her, I should decide what life if any to give her.

In July I finally made a decision on Usenda's future. It was the night of the fourth. I climbed up on to the roof of where I was staying in order to see the fireworks better. As I leaned back onto the roof I looked up to the night sky. I saw the beautiful display of colors as our country celebrated its freedom. I desperately wished my daughter and I could be part of that celebration.

Tears streamed down my face as I made the first and only decision as a mother. I felt and believed that bringing my daughter into a world of turmoil and conflict would not be the best idea.

I thought about how she might grow up and the person she might become. The struggles and problems she faced were overwhelming. I knew the world that she would live in would be one of turmoil. I didn't want my child to inherit my suffering. I wanted the rippling effect to stop with me. The thought of my circumstantial position in life rippling down and affecting someone else's entire life broke my heart. I knew at that very moment if I'd truly did love Usenda I had to let her go.

About one week, later I said goodbye to her and had an abortion. I don't feel my decision was selfish. To this day and my only regret is that society would not give us a chance for a different life together. I still stand firm, that I made the right choice for my daughter. It was not an easy decision, but I believe the right one. No one can persuade me to think or feel differently.

After I had the abortion, I started to make arrangements for the weeks ahead. My life of freedom was about to end, and I would be entering a new world living as someone with a past.

Two weeks before my court hearing; my Mom had finally got her wish to be able to help me. She drove down from New Mexico to help me pack my belongings in a storage unit at a place called Pac-n Stor.

I was only a shell of a person by then. I could not do much more than sleep because of the depression I had fallen into.

My Mother is a brave soul. I know the state I was in; and how my life being in shambles had to rip at her soul. You would not know it though. She kept every tear and sad emotion hidden from me.

She acted as though we were on a vacation at Disney Land; always laughing and joking; yet, knowing the whole time; that it might be years before she might see me again. She knew I did not need any more tragedy or tears. I was already pushed past the point of insanity. Another blow would have been more than I could handle.

I would like to believe I could be that strong minded, but in reality I don't think I would be able to.

Emotions of sadness held heavy in the air the day my Mom was leaving to go back to her home in New Mexico. I could sense her motherly instincts of protection. Behind her smile was the pain of not being able to protect one her offspring.

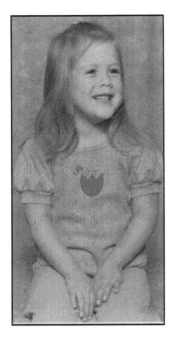

A small part of me too desperately wished, for a moment, that I was that little girl. We both knew I had to face the uncertain future alone.

Little did she know; that her fair well hug gave me the encouragement to find my way out of the darkness. As I watched her drive away I could see her eyes in her rear view mirror. She was watching me watch her.

"I promise to see you on the other side Mom," I whispered to myself, "I will be alright, you will see."

I knew somehow I would keep that silent promise to her. A mountain of despair lay ahead of me but I knew I could climb it. I just had to grasp whatever I could in order to get to the top.

That day was a turning point for me. At the time I could not see it but it was the day that I took my first step out of the core.

I had been homeless for over a year by the day I was to be sentenced at court. I felt like I had been at war with my own country and I had the scars to prove it. I was so tired by the time that day had come to life. Emotionally I was dead. I had no strength left inside myself to fight for my civil rights. Life and death held no concept to me. I did not want to die or live. I just wanted to have never been born. My

Right: My Mom (linda Dangberg) Left Myself

greatest desire and wish at that moment in life was to have never existed. I wanted to be as invisible as my country made me feel.

I no longer felt pain or fear. I was numb of all emotions. At that time in my life I didn't even feel hunger pains. Reality became such a blur. If there is a fine line between reality and imaginary a muddled mess replaced whatever line that did exist for me. By then, even cutting no longer kept me in focus of reality.

I came to a decision that no matter what happened; I was not going to be imprisoned for a crime that I obviously did not commit.

The morning of court I showered and dressed. Before putting on my sweater I took a permanent marker and wrote down both arms: 'I am innocent'. I then carefully hid two bottles of sleeping pills; in order to sneak them into the jail.

Looking up; I said aloud;"It is up to you if I live to see tomorrow."

My plan was if I was sentenced to prison I would ingest all the sleeping pills and die in the jail intake. That was my purpose for writing on my arms. I knew if I did die, what I wrote; would grabs someone's interest. My hope was that my death, would bring my innocence to life.

It was up to the judge if I was going to be sentenced to two years in prison as according to the agreement I had signed. My fate and future lay in the hands of one man.

I fortunately did not get prison time. The judge went against the plea bargain and gave me six months' in jail. I wasn't happy but I could live with that; at least it was not prison.

It was September 2004, when I was sentenced back into the chaotic world of jail. I just happen to be living under the scrutiny of the infamies Joe Arpio and his world renowned fame to the ill treated prisoners of tent city. I became one of many to have survived the horrific living conditions of tent jail.

September in Arizona is hot. It is much worse in June or July, but still none of the least, it is still a suffocating heat. I lived in a tent when I was homeless but I was not confined to the denim like clothing attire and I could get out of the heat when I felt I could no longer stand it. Another factor is I could drink whenever and whatever I wanted.

People who support tent city will protest and say the inmates are given water bottles. I do not deny that. What Joe's fan base neglect to say is that the contents in the bottles can and are regularly poured out for one reason or another. Now refilling it sounds simple and would be if you were allowed. Think back and remember I explained the term 'lock down'. I would now like to point out; that 'lock down,' can mean for hours of no water, food or bathroom breaks.

Joe Arpio's tent city is in my opinion a stomping ground of torment. We all heard his excuses a hundred times over and his famous saying of… "If you don't like it; then do not come here." And another famous saying of his goes something like; "This is jail; not the holiday inn."

I am not saying crime should go unpunished. But when cattle at a slaughter house are treated more humanely, than a human being; something is wrong with how our society has come to think of what is fair punishment.

I was given kitchen duty within the first month I was there. In less than a week I found out how the injured inmates are treated. Medical treatment there is at a minimal I discovered only after a suffering a serious accident while trying to pull a cart of dishes into the kitchen.

The cart became stuck in a doorway so another inmate tried to help by pushing it. It was stacked so high neither of us could see each other. As she pushed the cart it slipped and banged into the door frame. My right hand; happen to be resting on the cart and positioned in the right spot to collide into the metal frame. The webbing between my thumb and index finger was pinched off! The following morning I had close to twenty stitches carefully closing a wound that in the real world would recommend something other than stitching. Remember I said; the skin had been cut off, removed, so there was not much the poor medical personal could stitch.

I could go on and on about the horrors of tent city but I feel almost everyone has heard stories of what can go on in there. To me; that place has become another one of those circumstances that will continue to torment people until America says; **enough is enough**!! It happened to me and will continue to happen to another person until someone does something besides talk about how bad it is.

Figure 9 the next few pages are stories that I would like to share about tent city jail.

Inside America's toughest jail: Tent City, Arizona

More Phoenix Valley news: Ahwatukee | Central

By Eddi Trevizo Derek Cooley - Feb. 4, 2009 05:13 PM

The Arizona Republic .

Maricopa County Sheriff Joe Arpaio marched 220 chained illegal immigrant inmates into a segregated enclosure of Tent City Wednesday afternoon, despite protests from some County officials and civil rights groups who thought the procession violated human rights.

The 220 inmates walked from the Durango Jail complex to Tent City near 35th Avenue and Durango Street in Phoenix about 1 p.m. Wednesday. The inmates were chained at the feet and wore handcuffs while carrying bags full of personal belongings. The procession took about 15 minutes.

According to Arpaio the inmates will not be treated any differently than other inmates with two exceptions: Arpaio plans to have the inmates instructed in U.S. immigration law and have the inmates who violate jail rules put in a chain gang to work to clean areas of the Valley affected by human trafficking.

Protesters and some County officials believe the move was degrading and unnecessary.

"Shackling and marching fellow human beings for all to see is not in line with the values of the American people. While Guantanamo (Bay) is being closed, another one is being started in Arizona," Kevin Appleby, the Director of Migration and Refugee Policy with U.S. Conference of Catholic Bishops, said.

About 30 protesters gathered in front of the County Juvenile Court Center, near the Durango Jail complex, carrying signs that read "Human beings are not your circus animals" and "No more circus media.

"There is absolutely nothing dignified about marching illegal immigrants in chain gangs," Alessandra Soler Meetze,

executive director of the American Civil Liberties Union in Phoenix, said.

The inmates were transferred from the Durango Jail complex to an area of Tent City as a cost-cutting move, according to a statement released by the Maricopa County Sheriff's Office Tuesday.

However, protesters and Maricopa County Supervisor Mary Rose Wilcox said the cost-cutting effects of the move are negligible.

According to Wilcox, Arpaio has failed to submit a detailed budget-cutting proposal, despite a request made by the county's office of management to identify 20 percent of each department's budgets that could be cut.

Jack Kurtz/The Arizona Republic

Undocumented immigrant prisoners in the Durango Jail walk in chains and shackles to Tent City Feb. 4, 2009.

"He's trying to justify this as a 'budget savings,' and I'm just appalled. It's just another publicity stunt. He doesn't outline how he'll save costs," Wilcox said.

Despite the protesters' belief that the segregation and
separation of inmates is inhumane, separating inmates is not
unconstitutional unless the illegal inmates are treated differently
from other Tent City inmates, Meetze said.

Inmate separation is the exception and not the rule,
according to the Pima County Sheriff's Office and the El Paso
County Sheriff's Office in Texas. Both agencies experience a steady
flow of illegal immigrant detention. According to both agencies
crime severity and health issues are often the only criteria used to
separate inmates.

Inmates at the Pima County Jail are not separated based
on immigrant status or race, according to spokeswoman for the Pima
County, Dawn Barking.

"We separate the ones that cannot live with others because
of crime severity or mental issues," Jesse Tover, El Paso County
Sheriff's Office spokesman, said
(Kurtz)

hellnojoe - 9/18/09 1:56 AM - Report this

Report this:

I had 2 personal experiences in "Uncle Joe's" hell hole, due to inability to pay fines for driving infractions. The first time I was exposed to tuberculosis, and the second time I was violently ill with food poisoning.

As far as other inmates went, I was doing splendidly, because they actually let me see a medic, which was not done for the girl with a hole instead of a kneecap,(due to an untreated brown spider bite), or the girl the guards pushed out of a van.

This unfortunate girl didn't move fast enough, and although they transport you with chains clamped around your ankles, they pushed off while she was attempting to exit the back of the van. Being that she was the end girl on the chain, she must have broken her leg in more than one place because her leg looked more swollen than textbook cases of elephantitis.

I saw a woman so sick withdrawing from herion so sick all she could do is moan and shake. I noticed a huge infection oozing off her chin and jaw. I was told she was punched out by her boyfriend just prior to her arrest.

Her jaw appeared to be broken. I called for a nurse. One led her out and brought her back 5 minutes later with a little band aid on the tip of infection. I asked if she saw a doctor and she sobbed "no but they did give her an aspirin". She was one of the lucky ones.
(Unanamous, 2009)

Date: August 3, 2008

ARPAIO AND INMATES CELEBRATE
15TH ANNIVERSARY OF TENT CITY
With Plans to Build More Tents, Sheriff Concerned
Why Phoenix & Mesa Want to Build Their Own Jails

(Phoenix, AZ) It has been 15 years since Sheriff Joe Arpaio opened Tent City, the most unique and talked about jail in the country. Since its high noon opening on a very hot August 3, 1993, over 400,000 men and women have served their sentences in the Tents.

Tent City inmates have endured the broiling Arizona desert temperatures and below freezing temperatures in winter. Most inmates work inside the jail facilities while others serve time on the Sheriff's controversial chain gangs. Inmates have always been fed very low cost meals (average meal cost looms around 20 cents each) because of the Sheriff's aggressive search for inexpensive food items and gleaned products.

Yet even with these harsh, austere conditions, Tent City has enjoyed a largely trouble free existence in the past 15 years. Currently, the tents can hold 2,000 inmates and with expansion, the population can grow to approximately 2,500.

More tents are now being built in preparation for an influx of inmates coming from the state's new stricter DUI laws and an increase in jail bookings for other crimes, according to the Sheriff.

This time Sheriff Arpaio is looking to make Tent City a 'green' facility. Construction of the shower and toilet facilities for the new tent expansion will be operated by solar energy. The Sheriff is also examining other ways to make the jails environmentally friendly, and save taxpayer money, while still being tough on criminals.

Yet despite the success in Tent City and throughout the jails, the city officials of Phoenix and Mesa say they plan to build their own jails, a move that mystifies Arpaio. "Taxpayers are already

164

paying millions of dollars to operate our two brand new jails, which
the public voted for several years ago in a special sales tax. To my
mind, it's not good policy to ask them to pay higher taxes yet again
for more jails when we are doing fine with what we have," says the
Sheriff.

The authority to run the county's jails is given to the Sheriff
by the Arizona State Constitution. (MCSO, 2008)

Sherrif Joe's Chain gang burring the homeless

Chapter Six

(Pr

GIVING BACK

Upon being released from jail, I was ordered to live at a halfway house. I was willing to do anything by then to find normalcy again. I wanted happiness in my life and not turmoil. My only wish at that moment in my life was that someone; ...anyone, would have told me about a half way house when I first became homeless. I realized and understood that the half way house might be my only opportunity to a life I once lived.

Despite their rules; I knew my stubborn personality would not be accepted. I had to except my limitations and tolerate the half way house's wishes in order to move on with my life. Easy or not I swallowed my pride and abided by their rules.

When I was homeless, I felt as though no one cared to enough about my situation to even listen. Whatever happened to me was not a concern to anyone. Even though many times over I was the victim, I felt I was still at fault. I was made to believe I was nothing.

The half way house was my ticket to a life off the streets. During the long road in search of help I was a victim in many incidents. It was now my choice to go forward with my life. Until then I had been the victim but it was my choice to remain one.

I wanted to take everyone with me. I knew that thought was unrealistic, so instead I made a silent vow to one day be able to help someone like myself. (That silent promise became my driving force to success.)

I knew I had to let go of my street family, otherwise, I would always remain homeless. Not only did I have to let go of everything; I had to stop living for the moment and relearn to live with a future. I had to push everyone and everything I had come to know away from me. I had to let go all aspects of the streets. The knowledge that kept me alive no longer could exist.

Something deep down inside told me if I wanted a "normal" life again I had to walk, run, and hide from the streets. I isolated myself mentally, emotionally, and physically. I had to find myself again. I had to reconnect with that little girl who was lost and broken in a world of turmoil deep inside my soul.

When I found her I could not let her go. No matter what happened or who I emotionally conflicted with; I finally came first. For the first time in my life I made myself important.

Decisions made today can and will effect tomorrow. No matter how you try to forget, or how far you run, the past will affect you. I decided to make everyone else happy but myself. I would do almost anything to receive praise from others especially my family. I lost all sense of my individuality by becoming so hungry for love and praise.

I tried to hide from my past. Some decisions I made have turned into regrets. I tried to drink, smoke or cutting away my emotions. Today I let my scars and flaws become a part of me; they are who I am. I no longer try to please anyone but myself.

Drugs, alcohol, cutting, or any other measures thought of will only fix your feelings temporary.

The past is impossible to run from or forget. My past will probably always haunt me, but I have learned there is no way to run or hide from myself. I try to live with my demons. Some days they still torment me.

Sometimes I feel confused about decisions I have made. I wonder why I let myself be victimized repeatedly. I question many choices that I had made, and wonder what my reasoning at that time was. Where could my mind have been? Maybe now that I am older and wiser I rationalize events much differently than the outlandish youth who started on this walk. All I endured throughout the core has made me cautious and protective to what is left of me.

Unlike the wistful youth who began this journey, I know there are no knights in shining Armor. No longer do I waste my time or energy upon such frivolities. I know now, that the only footsteps I hear in hopes of a rescue, would be my own. I have learned my only rescuer to lean on would be me.

Someone who isn't so innocent to our nation's cruelty towards its most needy has replaced my naive self. When I was homeless, society made me feel so unimportant. I felt so undesirable and unworthy that, I no longer cared to look any one in their eyes. I felt inferior to everyone.

Deep down inside I knew I was just as worthy as anyone who belittled me. I knew I had to hold onto that belief or I would never be able to return to society. No matter how small I felt, I could not give up believing I deserve more. I was a victim, but it was my choice to remain one.

When I first arrived at the half way house, it was easy for me to not contact anyone I had come to have known, while living on the streets. The reason being I became agoraphobic due to post traumatic stress disorder. In simple terms, I was petrified to be out in public. I claimed the bedroom closet, as my space for the first week I lived there.

I quickly became friends with a shy, petite, blonde who was little on the heavy side due to have suffering the same thing I was. Her name was Linda and she became my saving angel. We were two broken souls that helped each other to heal. It is because of her that I can leave my house today.

I feel blessed, in having Linda come into my life. Our friendship is a bond that I will always carry with me. Unfortunately, she never got to see what she did for me, because she passed away, one year after I met her.

I refuse to let go those depressing memories today, because I know I would lose focus, on teaching others about the apparels of being homeless. What I endured, would be worth the loss, if I could empower just one person to help someone in need.

Today I am blessed to hold a place within society again. It feels good to have value and purpose. I don't take any day for granted anymore. I even treasure some of the downfalls life brings such as bills and schedules. I know that receiving a bill in the mail translates into having a roof over my head and someone out there found me worthy enough to bill me. I look at an empty cupboard as having a place to put more groceries into. On the days when I burn the candle at both ends and I cannot meet a deadline on my schedule; I know to be grateful for the stress.

The smallest thing you say or do could affect another person's life. The tiniest gesture could mean so much even though you might never imagine the impact something so insignificant could hold.

Two of the volunteers for the homeless count at the Hills Church in Phoenix, A

I met a woman named Seneca who in my eyes gave me a key to the world I live in now. She is a modest woman who would probably disagree with me and say what she does is not that much.

When I met her she was working at a place called St. Joseph the worker. I had just been released from jail and I was living at the half-way house. I finally conquered some of the fear people by then; crowded places still overwhelmed me a bit. She took that anxiety into consideration and gathered up information from me in order to write me a resume.. In my opinion, I feel she is a miracle worker. I do not know if she is aware that she did more than help me find that first step back into society. What she gave me was a building block that I have built upon over the years in order to be where I am today.

Two gentleman that I met in January 2007 during a homeless count at North Hills Church in Phoenix; I feel understand the impact one gesture could mean to someone. Both men had been through a lot in their lives. They had met in a recovery group and become good friends.

I had volunteered to help count the homeless. I found them to be delightful to be grouped with. We were given a desolate part of Phoenix to search for the homeless.

All three of us wanted to give something to someone that was living the life we had survived. All of us knew it was probably pointless to search desolate desert, but we all were determined to accomplish the task we had signed up for. We drove every mile and searched in the darkness finding no one. Unfortunately none of us got to physically help someone that night but we all felt good by trying to help. We went home hoping the information we had gathered would result in future assistance.

Upon receiving employment at Sky harbor air port; I started to give back to those who are still in the core I started an annual charity drive for a homeless school at my workplace. I enjoyed being able to give to those still struggling inside the core. I would tell fellow employees that the homeless could use their disregarded items more than goodwill.

I kept a little street knowledge with me as I became employed. Some knowledge that I learned on the streets has been helpful. Those long nights of dumpster diving and repairing merchandise to sell I discovered to be practical knowledge I applied at my place of employment. It saved my employer millions of dollars over the years I had worked in the ware house for Avila retail.

"Where did you learn how to fix things," my employer would ask in amazement.

"Life," I replied. I would then simply shrug my shoulders and smile.

Today; I spend a lot of my energy focusing on helping other people stuck in the core of their own hell on the streets. I know that you don't have to spend a penny to make someone happy.

I try to educate those who have never been there about the hopelessness of homelessness. Any one of every income level can do something for a homeless person. Even a glass of water on a hot day, would be appreciated by most homeless individuals.

I try to find a reason to why American's waste so much while others are going without. I have yet to understand that dilemma; maybe one day I will understand.

Although my hands remain disabled; I have learn to overcome my limitations and have returned to my passion of carving. I saw a blind man wood carving one day and thought to myself if he can do it ; I should be able to find a way as well.

I even got to experience the joy of showing some pieces in a gallery in Phoenix. I have yet to see a piece sell but I know that anything is possible.

When I was homeless, I might have thought otherwise, but after surviving my own core of hell I know never to under estimate the future.

As our economy goes into free fall, I hold onto to hope that my life won't go into a downward spiral as well. I sit on the edge of my seat, as I watch the news telling America how grim the job market has become. I feel that America's economy will continue in a down ward spiral until our society unites in this ongoing battle of homelessness.

Figure 10 two of the hundreds of Christmas ornaments I made in 2008.

Figure 11 a driftwood fountain I call 'Serenity'.

Figure 12 is a barstool I carved in 2007 called 'The Hunted'.

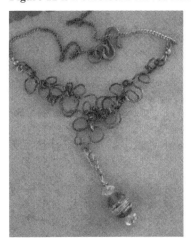

Figure 13 is a piece of jewelry I have made. This is a new creative outlet for me.

Top Picture: *Bobby (Survivor of Hurricane Katrina*
Bottom: *Myself (Survivor of circumstance)*

Top Photo: Two of the greatest guys I have met. (left) Sam and (right) Orlando.

Bottom Photo: (left) myself and (right) Sam

U.S. jobless figures hit 25-year high with 651,000 people laid off in one month

By _Mail Foreign Service_

Last updated at 2:00 PM on 06th March 2009

U.S. jobless figures hit a 25-year high today after employers axed 651,000 jobs in February.

While that figure was near economists' expectations for a 648,000 drop in non-farm payrolls, January and December job losses were revised sharply higher.

The Labor Department said the unemployment rate surged to 8.1 per cent in February, the highest level since December 1983.

ob _seekers wait in long lines to enter a career fair at a hotel in New York yesterday as unemployment figures rise in the U.S._

That was above market forecasts for a rise to 7.9 from January's 7.6 percent.

January's job cuts were revised to show a steep decline of 655,000, while December's payrolls losses were adjusted to 681,000, the deepest since October 1949.

Since the start of the recession in December 2007, the economy has purged 4.4 million jobs, with more than half occurring in the last 4 months.

Job losses in February were broad based, with only government, education and health services adding jobs.

'Since the recession began, the rise in unemployment has been concentrated among people who lost jobs, as opposed to job leavers or people joining the labor force,' said Bureau of Labor Statistics Commissioner Keith Hall.

The manufacturing sector shed 168,000 jobs in February, after eliminating 257,000 positions the prior month.

Construction industries bled 104,000 jobs in February after losing 118,000 in January.

The service-providing industry slashed 375,000 positions after shedding 276,000 in January.

With companies across all industries clobbered by weak consumer spending and loan defaults, the last thing investors want to hear is that Americans are getting laid off at a faster-than-anticipated pace.

As the economic crisis continues, many analysts believe there is little to keep stock from falling even further.

(Mail Foreign Service, 2009)

The last item I placed in my vehicle before pulling out of PAC-N Stor was a bible; that a friend had given me, after joining her church. As I drove out of the parking lot; my thoughts returned to the church congregations that I had met in the past.

If you are a Christian, could you still believe if life as you knew it was shattered? Could your faith withhold the ultimate test of strength? The homeless, in my opinion, know the answer to those questions. I feel homeless Christians are devout believers.

They are people who are suppressed. The lives they once lived and knew have been torn apart for one reason or another. The homeless are men, women, and children who have been displaced and their faith has been tested.

For those of you that claim to be a "good Christian," I ask, what does a person do for that title?   I have met people who claim that title. Some of those people that I have met I feel are hollow people with no clue to its meaning.

As I entered the center of the core, I met people who preached the bible and never listened to a word of what they had said. I have had churches turn their back to me. Whole congregations walked away when I cried out for help.

After going through the core, I have learned what the meaning of a "good Christian" should be. It is not just words in a book or a symbol worn around one's neck. Nor is it dressing to impress on Sundays.

A "good Christian" in my opinion is invisible kindness towards others. A title which is earned by a person being willing to uplift your brother or sister of humanity or caring enough to give a dying man your last piece of bread.

If you go to church look around and notice how many homeless people, you see. As you look, ask yourself if a homeless man or woman would be welcomed even if their appearance might not be appealing.

Now reach deep down inside your soul as you ask yourself if you could grab a homeless man or woman off the street and welcome him or her. Could you truthfully show mercy and compassion towards a dirty stranger on the street?

Many Christians claimed me as a lost soul when I was homeless. Losing everything materialistic made me find the true meaning of salvation. I believe I would never have truly been aware of its meaning otherwise.

I parked at several churches of all denominations in Phoenix, AZ. A couple of churches did reluctantly help me by allowing me to park in their parking lot. I feel most people would assume that parking in a big empty parking lot would not be a big deal. I thought so until I was literally chased out of some parking lots. In 2003, I started to distance myself from religion sanctions because of so many confrontations with church members. I stopped believing in church but kept I my faith. I was not going to let a few high and mighty Christians change what I grew up to believe.

I kept my distance from religious organizations until 2006. A friend had convinced me to try out their church. I drug my feet until I ran out of excuses and then finally reluctantly went to church with them. That church changed my opinion and resentment I held from the other churches. That church was North Hills Church. The congregation was so overwhelmingly friendly. The pastor was the person who made me become interested in the church again. His name was Pastor Steve. I found him to be so down to earth. He welcomed anyone without judgment or question. I started to go to that church almost every Sunday.

After eleven years of ministry at North Hills, Pastor Steve decided to retire. On the day he gave his last sermon, I realized I was blessed to have met such a unique Pastor. As I entered the church that morning, I could feel an air of sadness. Even before the service started, I could sense the passion his congregation had for everything that he had accomplished.

North Hills has grown and doubled in size over the eleven years that he was their pastor. The church itself has been rebuilt to accommodate the congregational growth. None of that mattered to Pastor Steve. He claimed his greatest accomplishment was the lives that he had changed.

With a beaming smile and raised arms he exclaimed, "How great God's Grace is and we all can be saved. You were not saved to sin, but saved to serve."

His voiced echoed in my head as I drove into a parking lot of a public park. I heard a familiar sound of a shopping cart as opened my car door and stepped out. I got out of my vehicle just in time to see a gentleman walk past me; pushing a shopping cart as he made his way up a driveway, leading to his house. A chuckle escaped me as I thought about their stereo types that I was once labeled with.

Early in my book, I pointed out the stereo types most homeless people receive upon losing their residences. I became most of those stereotypes, but I was none of them when I first landed on the streets of Phoenix. I didn't initially become a crazy person with a criminal record due to a shady past. I fought from becoming a society menace but lost. I was forced into becoming those stereotypes. Today I wonder how many others out there are like me, and how many more will American Society create before we say **enough is enough**!

It was a beautiful fall day as I continued to walk into the park and back into the shadows that haunt me still. I returned to where it all began. All thee insanity, thee inhumanity, and pain, I survived, flooded back to me; filling me up and surrounding my soul. Every incident, every cruelty, I endured; lunged at me. Tears of happiness and sorrow came to eyes and streamed down my cheeks finally realized; I was a survivor.

I had lost nothing in reality, but gained an education no one could ever teach. A lesson in life no one would dare walk while knowing what waited.

I looked around and saw myself amongst the homeless. My shadow remained there around them, but this time it was just my shadow; a fragment of memories etched by time now echoing silently in the past.

Finally, I understood; I was at last the outsider; looking in. I had made it back to the other side!!!! So many times in the past when I was homeless, I'd sit upon the grass and watch the people in the park. They all seemed so carefree; living life, and not having a clue how fortunate, they really were.

Children laughed sliding down the slippery side. "Watch me!! Watch me!!", squealed a little girl as she slid down one of the slides. Echoes of other children's voices and laughter could be heard as they played in the park.

Crowds gathered around picnic tables preparing for a traditional family outing. Smoke arose from nearby barbeque pits. Smells of chicken, hot-dogs and other wonderful picnic food aromas filled the air; yet intangible to myself.

Sometimes a cracking sound of a bat hitting a home- run could be heard from a nearby game. The sounds of cheering crowds would soon follow.

So many people of all sizes, shapes, and colors would pass by me. All of them; probably barely noticing me sitting on the grass in the shade, but I can still recall those memories today. I remember the women, the most especially the few who would dress in nice attire.

I would close my eyes listening to all the sounds, and smelling all the wonderful food and wishing I could open my eyes as one of the ladies in the park, trading places and misery. Unfortunately, when I reopened my eyes again; my misery would be the same and the women would always fade into their lives that I'd give anything to feel just for a second.

That night in Oct, I finally saw through their eyes and I faded into my life... knowing I made it through the core!!

Thank you for walking with me!!

Simple Advice

To the Invisible People;

This is a special note for anyone struggling within the core or knows someone who is. The next few pages are some tid –bits of information I was given on my way back.

I admit that I am not sure of how helpful they are but you might find the advice resourceful. I would like to make clear what works for one person doesn't always work for another.

My personal advice I will share is never give up, don't fall into quick fixes (drugs, alcohol, theft, ect.), and always remember society knows we are there; they would prefer not to admit it. YOU ARE NOT INVISIBLE!! Good luck and God Bless.

Fellow Comrade;

Stormi

PRAYER *for* SERENITY

God, grant me the serenity to accept
the things I cannot change,
courage to change the things I can
and wisdom to know the difference.

GOAL SETTING

My Long Term Goals. Where do I see myself in 6 months? What kind of work? What kind of living arrangement?

Goal 1:

Goal 2:

Goal 3:

My Short Term Goals. What can I start doing RIGHT NOW to make sure I'll be able to accomplish my long-term goals? These are the baby steps that I'll need to take first, or the pieces I have to put in place, to make long term goals achievable. Examples: ID, a job service, and recovery issues.

Goal 1:

Goal 2:

Goal 3:

St. Joseph the Worker
Job Services - Phoenix, Arizona

Our Mission

Our mission is to assist homeless, low-income and other disadvantaged individuals in their efforts to become self-sufficient through permanent, full-time employment.

St. Joseph the Worker's primary focus is helping people to help themselves. We provide people with the tools necessary to conduct successful job searches and support them in their efforts to better their lives.

St. Joseph the Worker is a small, privately funded 501(c) (3), non-profit organization located in the heart of downtown Phoenix, Arizona that has been operating since 1988.

Success

"St. Joseph the Worker concluded its fiscal year and is proud to report:

✦ 20 homeless and low-income individuals were assisted in securing full-time, sustainable employment.

✦ $9.50 an hour was the average starting pay rate for these individuals.

ª46% of the jobs secured offered benefits

ª656 individuals received comprehensive assistance, including one-on-one job-search assistance, job-readiness resources and referrals, *as well as encouragement and support to pursue a self-sufficient lifestyle.*

✦ *Additionally, 573 incarcerated individuals were taught job-search strategies and job-readiness to help them avoid homelessness or re-incarceration after their St. Joseph the Worker services include...*

ᵃ*One-on-one attention from a professional Job Developer*

✦ *Telephone/fax access to contact employers*

ᵃ*Mailing Address*

ᵃ*Job Readiness Workshop covering interviewing skills, personal presentation and communication, proper workplace etiquette and much more*

✦ *Frequently updated list of job openings*

✦ *Mock interviews*

✦ *Bus tickets to get to and from interviews and work*

✦ *Targeted services for previously incarcerated individuals to develop a job search strategy and effectively explain a criminal history or large gap in employment*

ᵃ*Reduced fare monthly bus passes for employed clients*

ᵃ*Résumé development*

ᵃ*Professional clothing and shoes*

✦ *Clothing/uniform and work tools upon verification of employment*

ᵃ*Housing and utility assistance*

ᵃ*Goal-setting and budgeting course*

✦ *Other services/assistance based on individual need*

Client Requirements and Responsibilities

Have two forms of identification (state-issued picture ID and social security card) upon registering

Be sheltered and not sleeping on the street - please call the emergency shelter hotline to find an open bed: 1-800-799-7739

Complete an application form in its entirety as one would for an employer

✦ *Attend an initial registration interview with a job developer*

Successfully complete the Job Readiness Workshop

Be alcohol/drug free for at least 30 days

Be dressed and ready for an interview when entering the office (as well as possible - we can assist with clothing for registered clients)

✦ *Use the office only when actively pursuing employment*

Check for mail and phone messages regularly

Provide verification of bus tickets used

Other Resources

St. Joseph the Worker is located on the <u>Human Services Campus</u>, a collaboration of about a dozen agencies designed to meet the needs of homeless individuals in Phoenix. Below are links to other providers on this unique Campus:

<u>Central Arizona Shelter Services</u>

<u>Lodestar Day Resource Center</u>

<u>Maricopa County Health Care for the Homeless</u>

<u>NOVA Safe Haven</u>

<u>St. Vincent de Paul</u>

Additional services in Phoenix that may be of assistance:

Andre House

Interfaith Cooperative Ministries

Friendly House

UMOM New Day Centers

Fresh Start Women's Foundation

Community Information and Referral

St. Joseph the Worker

Wish List

• *Employment Opportunities*

• *Men's gently used dress and khaki pants (sizes 30 to 34) and jeans (sizes 30 to 34)*

• *Men's gently used dress shoes (all sizes)*

• *Men's and women's gently used tennis shoes (all sizes)*

• *Men's and women's new socks (dress and standard white)*

• *Men's new underwear (all sizes) and new undershirts (standard, v-neck, tank)*

• *Women's new underwear (all sizes) and brassieres*

• *Men's new or gently used belts*

• *Men's new or gently used pants (all sizes)*

• *Women's new pantyhose*

• *Men's new or gently used wallets*

• *Razors, toothbrushes and hairspray*

• *Sewing Kits*

• *Day planners*

• *Quality, durable 2-pocket folders*

• *Copy paper*

• *Coffee (larger cans/ any brand), creamer and sugar*

• *Styrofoam cups*

• *Hardware/grocery store gift cards*

• *Financial support, gifts of stock*

St. Joseph the Worker is located on the Human Services Campus in downtown Phoenix at 1125 West Jackson Street.

Donations may be dropped-off at our office anytime during M-F from 7a.m. to 4 p.m. Below are detailed directions

to St. Joseph the Worker. If you have any questions, please do not hesitate to contact us at 602-417-9854. Thank

you for considering St. Joseph the Worker and we look forward to seeing you soon.

Directions to St. Joseph the Worker on the Human Services Campus:

1. From I-10, exit 7th Avenue and go South

2. Turn right (or West) onto Washington (one-way street)

3. Turn left (or South) onto 9th Avenue

4. Pass Jefferson (next main street), pass Madison (stop sign), and turn right (or West) onto Jackson St.

5. Look for steel black gate on left hand side that says "Volunteer/Visitor Entrance"

6. Enter code 62339 on the key pad next to the black box. If there is difficulty entering the gate ,call 602-417-9854 and we will get you through.

7. Enter parking lot, turn right behind the blue building, park behind the second building (gray)

8. Hit page button on the black box next to the door with the St. Joseph the Worker sign

9. Call 602-417-9854 with any questions.

"Working to End Homelessness"

St. Joseph the Worker

Assisting homeless, low-income and other disadvantaged individuals in their
(Worker)

What's my personality type?

An additional way to understand yourself is to look at your personality type in relation to your interest areas and work style.

Outdoor/Mechanical	Science/Technical	Arts/Communication
"Doers"	"Thinkers"	"Creators"

ARE YOU....	ARE YOU....	ARE YOU....
Practical Athletic	inquisitive analytical	creative intuitive
Frank Mechanical	scientific observant	imaginative innovative
Nature lover Thrifty	precise scholarly	unconventional emotional
Curious Stable	cautious curious	independent expressive
Concrete Reserved	self-confident introspective	original impulsive
Self-controlled Ambitious	reserved broadminded	sensitive open
Systematic Persistent	independent logical	complicated idealistic

CAN YOU....	CAN YOU....	CAN YOU....
Fix electrical things	Think abstractly	sketch, draw, paint
Play a sport	Solve math problems	play a musical instrument
Read a blueprint	Understand scientific theories	write stories, poetry, music
Pitch a tent	Do complex calculations	sing, act, dance
Plant a garden	Use a microscope or computer	design fashions or interiors
Operate tools and machinery	Interpret formulas	

Do you like to....	Do you like to....	Do you like to....
Tinker with machines	explore a variety of ideas	attend concerts, theaters
Vehicles	use computers	read fiction, plays, poetry
Work outdoors	work independently	work on crafts
Be physically active	perform lab experiments	take photographs
Use your hands	read scientific or technical journals	express yourself creatively
Build things	analyze data	deal with ambiguous ideas
Tend/train animals	do research	
Work on electronic equipment	be challenged	

Social/Personal		Sales/Management		Business Operations	
"Helpers"		"Persuaders"		"Organizers"	
ARE YOU....		ARE YOU....		ARE YOU.....	
Friendly	Helpful	Self Confident	Assertive	Well-organized	Accurate
Idealistic	Insightful	Sociable	Persuasive	Methodical	Polite
Outgoing	Understanding	Enthusiastic	Energetic	Conscientious	Efficient
Cooperative	Generous	Adventurous	Popular	Conforming	Orderly
Responsible	Forgiving	Impulsive	Ambitious	Practical	Thrifty
Patient	Empathetic	Inquisitive	Agreeable	Systematic	Structured
Kind	Persuasive	Talkative	Extroverted	Ambitious	Obediant

\N YOU...

Teach/train others
Express yourself clearly
Lead a group discussion
Mediate disputes
Plan and supervise an activity
Cooperate well with other

CAN YOU....

Initiate projects
Convince people to do things your way
Sell things or promote ideas
Give talks or speeches
Lead a group
Persuade others

CAN YOU...

Work well within a system
Do a lot of paperwork fast
Keep accurate records
Use a computer
Write effective letters

Do you like to....

Work in groups
Help people with problems
Participate in meetings
Do volunteer work
Work with young people
Play team sports
Serve others

Do you like to.....

Make decisions affecting others
Be elected to office
Win a leadership or sales award
Start you own service or business
Campaign politically
Meet important people
Have power or status

Do you like to...

Work with numbers
Type
Be responsible for details
Collect or organize things
Follow clearly defined
procedures
Use data processing
equipment

HINTS FOR THE APPLICATION

1. Unless you were referred by someone within the company or who works with the company put down "company reputation".

2. Remember to put the area code with the phone number.

3. Fill in all gaps of time. Include any work you might have done while in prison. The employer would be the state in which you were incarcerated. Ex: State of Arizona, P.O. Box, city and zip code. The reason you ended that job if released is moved or relocated. You can also put down "contract ended" which is good if you switched to a different job.

4. If there was a period of time you did odd jobs here and there to make money, add those dates together to get one lump sum of time and for employer put "self-employed".

5. Try to fill all 4-job listings.

6. Under education, read to make sure you begin with high school or the most recent school you attended.

7. List skills you have that are most relevant to the position you are applying for.

8. Under conviction, if it is yes be sure to check it and put "will explain in interview".

9. It is okay to give an out of town reference but be sure to get permission from your references before you put their down, then notify them when you apply.

A SCRIPT FOR EXPLAINING A CONVICTION

Employer: "I see you marked that you have a conviction. Can you tell me a little more about that?"

Ex-Offender: "Yes, I'd be happy to explain that to you because I want you to feel perfectly comfortable in hiring me. When I was younger, _____(A)_____ But now, _____(B)_____ I am eager to show you what I can do.

(A) Your conviction, any conviction, can be explained in just a sentence or two. The following are a couple instances:
1. Drugs or drug related crimes:
   When I was younger I abused substances, but I have been clean and sober now for _____.
2. Theft:
   When I was younger, I took something that didn't belong to me.
3. Assault:
   When I was younger, I was involved in a physical altercation.

One sentence briefly and honestly tells the employer what the conviction was about. They may ask for more details for instance, "what did you take?" You can briefly answer a car, money, etc. But continuing with part (B) will put the attention on the more positive aspects.

Examples

(B) 1. Drug related crimes:
   In the past I was involved with drugs, but since that time I have been living . . substance abuse recovery house. I have been clean and sober for _____ I've been able to go back and get a GED. I have _____ years experience in (ex: clerical work) and can (ex: type 35 wpm/10 key/answer 5 lines). I am eager to show you what I can do.
2. Theft:
   "I took something that didn't belong to me, but since that time I've been certified to drive a forklift."

You want to include:
- any schooling or certificate you've earned both outside or while in prison
- any work experience you gained inside or since you've been out
- any substance abuse, anger management, parenting or other classes you might have taken or are taking

End with the related skills you have for the particular job you are interviewing for and:
"I am eager to show you what I can do."

JOB INTERVIEW TIPS

- Bring only essential items to the interview (i.e., resume, references, portfolio, licenses, datebook, etc.) Do not bring anything unrelated to the job into the interview.

- Arrive 15 minutes early so you can relax and review what you want to say.

- Be pleasant and friendly but businesslike to everyone you meet.

- Shake hands firmly. Be yourself. Use natural gestures and movements.

- Stress your qualifications without exaggeration. Emphasize experience and training related to the job opening.

- If you know about the company's products and services, you should refer to them as you answer questions. It is impressive if you have positive knowledge about the company. If the company is involved in any kind of problem (i.e., lawsuits, layoffs, etc.) do not bring it up.

- After being asked a question, it is okay to pause and think about your answer. Answer questions with more than a "yes" or "no." On the other hand, do not ramble. A successful interview occurs if the interviewer talks fifty-percent of the time.

- Speak positively of past employers and avoid discussing personal, domestic or financial problems.

- Know your salary range from your research. When asked "What are your ideas on salary?," answer with a question of the interviewer. i.e., "What do you pay people with my skills and experience?"

- Ask probing questions about the company plans, nature of the job, etc. Questions indicate interest and motivation. Questions are also helpful in getting the interviewer to talk.

- Be prepared if the interviewer says, "You're perfect for this job. When can you start?" Preparing for this question can prevent a snap decision. Most employers will allow you time to make this decision. But – what if they ask, "Can you start tomorrow?"

- Thank the interviewer even if they indicate that you are not right for the job. Ask about other companies that might be hiring. Get a name of someone to see.

- Send a brief thank you note immediately after the interview.

- Call a few days after the interview to see if a hiring decision has been made.

view. The following are some suggestions from experienced interviewers.

- Allow things to happen.
  Relax. Don't feel you have to start a serious interview right away. Go with the chitchat, if that is what the employer wants to do.
- Smile.
  Look and sound happy to be there and to meet the interviewer.
- Use the interviewer's name.
  Be formal. Use "Mister Rogers" or "Ms. Evans" unless you are asked to use another name. Use his or her name as often as you can in your conversation.
- Compliment something in the interviewer's office.
  Look for something you can compliment or something you have in common. Most offices have photographs or other things you can comment on. Say how great her kids look or ask whether he decorated the office himself.
- Ask some opening questions.
  After a few minutes of friendly talk, you could ask a question to get things started. For example:
  "I'd like to know more about what your organization does. Would you mind telling me?"
  or
  "I have a background in _____ and I'm interested in how these skills might best be used in an organization such as yours."

Some Self-Improvement Notes

Consider what you have learned about Phase 2 of an interview and note any specific ideas to improve your interview performance.

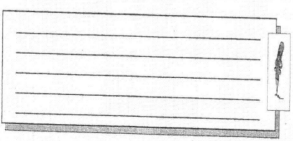

Interviewers react to many things you say and do during the first few minutes of an interview. Here are some of the things they mention most often:

Initial Greeting

Be ready for a friendly greeting! Show you are happy to be there. Although this is a business meeting, your social skills will be considered, too. A firm, but not crushing, handshake is needed unless the interviewer does not offer to shake hands. Use her last name in your greeting if possible, as in "It's good to meet you Ms. Kelly." And make sure you get her name and status technically and politically correct! This might require you to call in advance to make sure.

Posture

How you stand and sit can make a difference. You look more interested if you lean forward in your chair when talking or listening. If you lean back, you may look too relaxed.

Voice

You may be nervous, but try to sound enthusiastic and friendly. Your voice should be neither too soft nor too loud. Practice sounding confident.

Eye Contact

People who don't look at a speaker's eyes are considered shy, insecure, and even dishonest. Although you should never stare, you look more confident when you look at the interviewer's eyes while you listen or speak. Don't stare, of course.

Distracting Habits

You may have nervous habits you don't even notice. But pay attention! Most interviewers find such habits annoying. For example, do you:

- ✔ Play with your hair or clothing?
- ✔ Say something like "You know?" or "Uhh" over and over?
  ("*Uhh, you know what I mean?*")

The best way to see yourself as others do is to have someone videotape you while you role-play an interview. If that is not possible, become aware of how others see you, and then try to change your negative behavior. Your friends and relatives also can help you notice annoying habits you have that could bother an interviewer.

Establishing the Relationship

Almost all interviews begin with informal chitchat. Favorite subjects are the weather, whether you had any trouble getting there, and similar topics. This informal talk seems to have nothing to do with the interview; but it does. These first

- **Colognes, aftershaves, make-up, jewelry:**
  Again, be conservative. Keep your makeup simple and avoid too much of anything. Use perfumes or colognes lightly or not at all.
- **Careful grooming is a must:**
  Get those hands and nails extra clean and manicured. Eliminate stray facial hairs. Get a simple hair style.
- **Spend some money if necessary:**
  Get one well-fitting "interview outfit." Get your hair styled. Look a bit sharper than you usually do. If you have a limited budget, borrow something that looks good on you! It's that important.
- **Consider using a "uniform":**
  Some styles are almost always acceptable in certain jobs. For men working in an office, a conservative business suit, white shirt, and conservative tie are always acceptable. A less formal approach would include gray slacks, a blue blazer, white or blue shirt, and a conservative tie. For women, there are many more alternatives, but a simple tailored skirt, matching jacket, and white blouse are a safe choice. Women should not wear informal clothing to a job interview.
- **Dress up, not down:**
  In jobs that don't require formal dress, plan to dress a few notches above the clothing you might normally wear in that job. You can, of course, overdress for an interview too. That's why my Rule for Interview Dress and Grooming is so important.
- **Ask for advice:**
  If you are not sure how to dress and groom for an interview, discuss proper interview dress and grooming with friends *(who have a good sense of style)* and family *(if you dare)* before you finally decide for yourself. You also can get good books at the library that give helpful tips for "dressing for success." And the staff at many full-service clothing stores may be able to give you advice.

After you've thought about it, write how you plan to dress and groom for an interview in the spaces below.

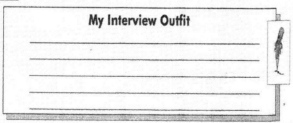

My Interview Outfit

Fresh Start
Women's Foundation

Getting Started

Center Overview

Fresh Start Women's Foundation is a nonprofit organization dedicated to helping women help themselves. We do that through the work of the Jewell McFarland Lewis-Fresh Start Women's Resource Center.

Our History

The Inspiration for Fresh Start

Pat Petznick and Beverly Stewart were inspired to create a women's organization, in tribute to the life of their paternal grandmother, Autie Jones. Autie was only 29 when her husband died of tuberculosis, leaving her to raise their young boys ages 1, 2 and 3. There were no relatives nearby to lend support, so she kept her family together by living in the back room of a grocery store where she worked. By day, she was a store clerk and at night, she shared precious moments with her sons while ironing other's clothes. Within a year, sadly her oldest son also died. Autie's life was full of financial and emotional hardship, yet she courageously chose to celebrate the blessings of every situation. This courageous woman was the inspiration for her granddaughters to reach out to women who struggle to survive. Fresh Start was born as a result.

The Foundation is Formed

Mission: Fresh Start is dedicated to helping women help themselves.

In 1995 the sisters formalized a foundation and established their first Board of Directors. In the early years, the foundation focused on fundraising and granting money to Arizona nonprofits serving women in need. Through the course of that granting process it became apparent there were gaps in the services for women being offered in our community. First, the Mentoring Program was formed and as a result then finally, the Women's Resource Center. As the organization grew, two new boards were added bringing an impressive array or community leaders to the effort.

Our Stories

Fresh Start Women's Foundation is dedicated to helping women help themselves. Most of the women we see are women with transitional needs. They are women just like you, who have either been dealt a devastating blow or simply want to improve their quality of life.

If any of these situations sound like something you are currently experiencing, stop by the Jewell McFarland Lewis - Fresh Start Women's Resource Center today. We can help. All women are welcome and most services are at no-charge.

- Going through a divorce
- Out of work
- Relationship issues
- Need a better job
- Recently widowed
- Parenting issues
- Living with abuse
- Recently single
- Self-esteem issues
- Need help accessing resources in the community
- Would like a mentor
- Stuck in a dead-end job
- Can't make ends meet
- Credit problems
- Need legal help on family law matters
- Self improvement help
- Starting a business
- Health and wellness issues
- Interested in personal growth
- Need the support of a group

Fresh Start serves all women. (Foundation)

North Hills

15025 North 19th Avenue, Phoenix, AZ 85023 |
602.863.6040

Welcome to North Hills Church, where everyone is important and accepted as you are.

If you are new to North Hills and want to check us out, we invite you to come and be a part of our many on-campus experiences. Our hope is that you would resonate with our relaxed family atmosphere, and our desire to connect with people in a very relevant way. We would love to meet you and have you experience what God is doing in our church community. At North Hills Church, there is a place for you.

Our Vision, Values, and Beliefs

Once we have connected with God, we have a simple vision:

CONNECT, SERVE, and IMPACT our Community with the good news and life of Jesus.

We aim to:
- CONNECT with people where they are;
- SERVE them at their point of need; and
- IMPACT them with the love and grace of Jesus!

Our ministry values give focus to our vision. We seek to staff, resource, equips, and encourage our members in these vital areas:

•Worship: Experiencing God's presence through the teaching of His Word and encountering Him through worship. We believe this weekly experience is life-giving and essential to God's children.

•Discipleship: Going deeper in God's Word and in fellowship as a church family through small group bible studies in both on and off-campus settings.

•*Family: Championing the sanctity of marriage and family. We recognize the many faces of the family of God - young and old, single, divorced, coming from all backgrounds.*

•*Life Care: Meeting needs in the family of God. No one should feel alone as they go through the struggles of life.*

•*Outreach: Reaching out and meeting real needs of real people in a real world.*

Our History

North Hills Church has been effectively communicating the life changing message of Jesus Christ to the greater Phoenix community since 1907.   The congregation has enjoyed this impressive tenure of effective ministry by maintaining a relevant message, and reinventing itself to meet the needs of upcoming generational cultures. With a long history of strong Pastoral leadership in Preaching/Teaching and Music/Worship Arts, North Hills has developed a high level of excellence in a variety of ministry programs. With a dedicated core of family members, this congregation will have a bright future well into the next century.

Various Shelters In the United States

Washington

Benton Franklin Community Action Committee (509)545-4042 720
W Court Street Pasco, WA 99301
Emergency Shelter Pasco Shelters

Bread & Roses Hospitality House   (360)754-4085
1320 8th Ave Se Olympia, WA 98501
Emergency Shelter for women/families with children

Bread of Life Mission   (206) 682-3579
97 South Main St Seattle, WA 98194
i have volunteered at this shelter. they provide over 200 meals a day.
they have 60 beds, showers, clothing, and rehabilitation services.

Central Area Motivation Program   (206)812-4952/(
722 18th Ave. Seattle, WA 98122
Emergency cold-weather motel vouchers during winter months
(November to March) for families with children under 18.

Community Action Center   (509)334-9147
350 S E Fairmont Road Pullman, WA 99163
Emergency Shelter

Council for the Homeless   (360)993-9561
2500 Main Street Vancouver, WA 98660
Referrals Advocacy Outreach Services

First Avenue Service Center Family Center   (206)441-8405
2013 Third Avenue. Seattle, WA 98104
Emergency day shelter for families with children under 18.
Mason County Homeless Shelter   (360)427-6919

212 N 1st St. Shelton, WA 98584

Emergency Shelter.

Multi-Service Center & Shelter   (253)838-6810

1200 S 336th St. Federal Way, WA 98003

Emergency Shelter Days only

Noel House Women's Referral Center   (206)441-3210

2325 Fourth Ave. Seattle, WA 98121

Women only shelter 18+ 40 beds referrals to other shelters.

Oasis Teen Shelter   360-419-9058

125 North Fift Street Mount Vernon, WA 98273

We are an Emergency overnight shelter servicing teens aged 13-17.
The shelter is open daily from 4pm to 8:30 am the following day. The
shelter has six beds, and runs on a first come, first serve basis. Teens
can stay for up to 21 days.

Olympic Community Action Programs   (360)385-2571

823 Commerce Loop Port Townsend, WA 98368

Advocacy

Opportunity Council   (360) 679-6577

1791 NE 1st Ave Oak Harbor, WA 98277

Prison Mission Association   (206)876-0489

1774 South East Vale Road Port Orchard, WA 98366   Family shelter

24-Hour Oakland Parent Teacher Children's Center   (510) 532-0574

4700 International Boulevard Oakland, CA 94601

Shelter for families

California

American Red Cross of the Bay Area   (415) 427-8000

85 Second Street 8th Floor San Francisco, CA 94105   Mass Shelter

Anka Behavioral Health   (888) 873-7463
1875 Willow Pass Road Suite 300 Concord, CA 94520
Homeless Mentally Ill

Asian Women's Home   (408) 975-2739
240 Moorpark Ave. Ste. 300 San Jose, CA 95128
Domestic Violence

Asian Women's Shelter (AWS)   (877) 751-0880
3543-18th Street Suite 19 San Francisco, CA 94110
Women Shelter

BOSS Multi Agency Service Center (MASC)   (510) 843-3700
1931 Center Street Berkeley, CA 94704   Homeless Teens

Bakersfield Homeless Center   661-322-9199
1600 East Truxtun Ave Bakersfield, CA 93305
174 Bed Shelter Families & Single Women Single Fathers allowed
Boys over 12 years allowed

Bay Area Rescue Mission - Men's Shelter   (510) 215-4868
200 MacDonald Avenue Richmond, CA 94801
Mens Shelter

Bay Area Rescue Mission - Women/Family Shelter   (510) 215-4860
224 MacDonald Avenue Richmond, CA 94801
Shelter Women with children

Berkeley Food and Housing Project   (510) 649-4965
2140 Dwight Way Berkeley, CA 94704

They have eight different programs which range from free evening meals to permanent supportive housing. Men's overnight shelter (50 bed 60 day shelter), women's overnight shelter, women's resource cen

Beth-El Baptist Church Outreach   (408) 779-2300
810 Tennant Avenue San Jose, CA

Bridgehouse Homeless Shelter   (805) 737-9449
2025 Sweeney Lompoc, CA 93436
Shelters

Cameron House   (415) 781-0401
920 Sacramento Street SAN FRANCISCO, CA 94108
Women Shelter

Casa Youth Shelter   (562) 594-6825
10911 Reagan Street Los Alamitos, CA 90720
Domestic Violence Shelters

Casa de Clara   (408) 297-8330
318 N. 6th St. San Jose, CA 95112   Families

Cassidy Program for Homeless Seniors - Brentwood - CCEB
(925) 308-7775
654 Third Street Brentwood, CA 94513   Homeless Mentally Ill

Cassidy Program for Homeless Seniors - Concord - CCEB   (925)
825-3099
3540 Chestnut Concord, CA 94519   Homeless Mentally Il

Central County Interim Housing Program - Concord Shelter   (800)
799-6599
2047 Arnold Industrial Way Concord, CA 94520   Men's Shelter

Child Abuse Prevention Center   (650) 688-1900
408 Sherman Avenue Palo Alto, CA 94306

City Team Ministry Rescue Mission   (408) 283-2153
1174 Old Bayshore Hwy. San Jose, CA 95112
Men/Women

Coastside Opportunity Center   (650) 726-9071
99 Avenue Alhambra PO Box 1089 El Granada, CA 94018
Families

Community Housing & Shelter Services   (209) 574-1149
823 15th Street Modesto, CA 95354
Homeless Services

Community Housing Partnership   (415) 391-2404
810 Avenue D San Francisco, CA 94130

Community Housing Partnership   (415) 749-1695
835 Ofarrell Street San Francisco, CA 9410

Community Revitalization Corporation   (530) 221-6960
2051 Hilltop Drive Redding, CA 96002

Community Solutions   (408) 846-4700
Homeless Youth (Pregnant & Parenting) 6980 Chestnut Street, CA

Community Solutions   408-846-4700
Transitional Housing Program (THP) 16264 Church St. Suite 10, CA

Community Working Group
555 Bryant Street Palo Alto, CA   (650) 562-3888

Compass Community Services   (415) 399-9406

995 Market Street 5th Floor San Francisco, CA 94103

Del Richardson & Assoc Inc   (909) 629-4194
600 South Towne Avenue Pomona, CA 91766

Deliverance House   (510) 215-1204
113 MacDonald Avenue Richmond, CA 94801   Men's Shelter

Dimondale Adolescent   (562) 494-7534
1461 North Anaheim Place Long Beach, CA 90804
Homeless Services

Dimondale Adolescent   (323) 777-6258
2509 West 115th Place Hawthorne, CA 90250
Homeless Services

Dream Catcher Youth Shelter and Support Center   (510) 522-8363
422 Jefferson Street Alameda, CA 94607
Shelter Runaway Youth

EHC LifeBuilders James Boccardo Reception Center (BRC) Nightly
Shelter   95125
2011 Little Orchard Stree San Jose, CA
(408) 294-2100 x 402 (Intake Coordinator)

EHC LifeBuilders Markham Terrace Permanent
2112 Monterey Road San Jose, CA
(408) 294-2100 Ext. 229 (Application)

EHC Lifebuilders Boccardo Family Living Center   (408) 686-
1300
13545 Monterey Road San Jose, CA

Ecumenical Hunger Program   (650) 323-7781

2411 Pulgas Avenue Palo Alto, CA 94303   Homeless Services

Emergency Shelter Program
22634 Second Street #205 Hayward, CA 94541
(510)581-5626

Emmanuel Outreach Temple Inc.   (714) 773-1008
1335 W Valencia Dr Fullerton, CA 92833
Homeless Services

Enlightment Last Chance   (951) 943-3590
21200 Old Elsinre Road Perris, CA 92570   Shelters

Eoc-Economic Opportunity Commission - Program Offices   (805)
466-5795
EOC Homeless Services Atascadero, CA 93422
Homeless Services

Exceptional Childrens Foundation   (310) 559-0922
10918 Barman Avenue Culver City, CA 90230   Homeless Services

FESCO - The Family Shelter   (510) 581-3223
22671 Third Street Hayward, CA 94541   Shelter men with children
    Families in Transition   (831) 458-7124
210 High St. Ste. 105 Santa Cruz, CA 95060
Families

First Step Transitional Living Foundation   323-285-7188
6214 S. Western Ave Los Angeles, CA 90047
Transitional Housing for highly motivated people, plus job
opportunities available

GOOD NITE   760 908-3525
13361 NAVAJO RD APPLE VALLEY, CA 92308

GRIP Family Housing Program   (510) 233-2141
165 - 22nd Street Richmond, CA 94801   Shelter family

Global Children's Organization   Homeless Servic
Santa Monica CA, CA (310) 581-2234

Global Human Service Inc   (818) 507-6026
434 West Cypress Street Glendale, CA 91204

Guerrero House - Catholic Charities   (415) 550-4478
899 Guerrero Street San Francisco, CA 94110
Men's Shelter

H O W Foundation   (562) 218-3035
1870 Myrtle Avenue Long Beach, CA 90806
Homeless Services

Habitat For Humanity   (818) 899-6180
11257 Borden Avenue Pacoima, CA 91331
Homeless Services
Haley House   (760) 255-3193
105 North 7th Avenue Barstow, CA 92311 Domestic Violence

Health Connections AIDS Services   (408) 961-9850
1701-A S. Bascom Ave. Campbell, CA 95008   Men/Women

Health Connections AIDS Services   (800) 683-1417
7365 Monterey St. Ste. C Gilroy, CA 95020   Families

Health Housing and Integrated Service Network (HHISN) -Pittsburg
need phone number
550 School Street suite 50 Pittsburg, CA 94565 homeless Individuals

Nebraska

Columbus Rescue Mission   402-563-1096

1471 25th Ave Columbus, NE 68601

Homeless shelter is a 2 week overnight program. Meals are provided. Call for details.

Crossroads Center Rescue Mission   (402) 462-6460

702 W 14th St Hastings, NE 68901

Established in 1983 as a soup kitchen, Crossroads is now a 90-bed facility with a four-phase program to help homeless men, women & families get back on their feet. We are located in Hastings, Nebraska. Our mission is to bring glory to God through the helping of people.

Jacob Rand Day Room   402-422-1111

2828 N. 23rd St. East Omaha, NE 68108

Day center for homeless men with physical or mental disabilities. Laundry, computers, medical services provided.

Open Door Mission   (402)422-1111

PO Box 19345 Omaha, NE 68119

Provides help for homeless men. Bible classes, life skills classes, computer learning classes.

People's City Mission   (402)475-1303

110 Q Street Lincoln, NE 68501

Homless shelter for men. Provides meals, clothing, laundry, chapel services, mail, etc

Siena Francis House   (402) 341-1821

1702 Nicholas Street Omaha, NE 68102

Largest homeless shelter in Nebraska. For all homeless. Call for details.

Illinois

Cornerstone Community Outreach   773.506.6396
4615 North Clifton Ave Chicago, IL 60640

Lincoln Park Community Shelter   (773) 549-6111
600 W Fullerton Pkwy Chicago, IL

Yazz Women & Children Fund   773 874 4000
80 Langley chicago, IL 60619
childrenfund.com

Breakthrough Urban Ministries - Women's Services   (773)722-0179
3330 W. Carroll Ave. Chicago, IL 60624

Breakthrough Urban Ministries Inc. Men's Services   (773)346-1785
402 North St Louis Chicago, IL 60624

Community Renewal Society   (312)588-0171
322 S Michigan Avenue #500 Chicago, IL 60604

Deborah's Place   (773)722-5080
2822 West Jackson Blvd. Chicago, IL 60612

Heartland Alliance for Human Needs & Human Right(312)660-1386
208 South LaSalle Street Chicago, IL 60604

Howard Area Community Center   (773)262-6622
7638-48 N Paulina Street Chicago, IL 60626

Interfaith House   (773)533-6013
3465 W. Franklin Boulevard Chicago, IL 60624

Pacific Garden Mission   (312)922-1462

1458 S Canal St Chicago, IL 60605

Residents for Effective Shelter Transitions (REST)   (773)784-0909
5253 N. Kenmore St. Chicago, IL 60640

Sousa Homeless Shelters   (773)874-4000
7000 S. Aberdeen Street Chicago, IL 60621

St. Martin de Porres House of Hope Inc.   (773)643-5843
6423 South Woodlawn Avenue Chicago, IL 60644

The Ark   (773)973-1000
6450 N Califormia Avenue Chicago, IL 60645

Arizona

Bread of Life Mission of Holbrook   928-524 3874
885 Hermosa Drive Holbrook, AZ 86025
Separate shelters for men and for women/families

Brewster Center for Victims of Family Violence   (602)880-7201
2711 E. Broadway Tucson, AZ 85716   Shelter for Families

Casa del los Ninos   520-624-5600
1101 N. 4th Avenue Tucson, AZ 85705   Women & children

Central AZ Shelter Services   (602) 256-6945
1209 W Madison St Phoenix, AZ 85007

Cochise County Children's Crisis Center - Open Inn   877-520-8336
721 Gonzales Blvd Huachuca City, AZ 85616
This is an emergency shelter in Cochise County for children under 17
years of age.

Cornerstone Mission   928-757-1535

3049 Sycamore Avenue Kingman, AZ 86401

Families/Single

Crisis Nursery   (602) 273-7363

2711 E. Roosevelt Phoenix, AZ 85008   children

Crossroads Mission   928-783-9362

944 S. AZ Avenue Yuma, AZ 85364   Shelter for Families

Crossroads Nogales Mission   520-287-5828

456 N Morley Nogales, AZ 85621   Shelter for Men

Louisiana

A NEW INSPIRATION   (225) 343-3286

1272 LAUREL ST. BATON ROUGE, LA

ACADIANA RECOVERY CENTER   (337) 291-5400

401 W. VERMILION STREET LAFAYETTE, LA

ACC/CARE CENTER   (504) 822-3751,

4222 SOUTH BROAD STREET NEW ORLEANS, LA

ACC/CRESCENT HOUSE I   (504) 865-0057,

CONFIDENTIAL NEW ORLEANS, LA

ACC/CRESCENT HOUSE II   (504) 865-0057,

CONFIDENTIAL NEW ORLEANS, LA

ACC/JEFFERSON PARISH CARE CENTER   (504) 347-0772,

1108 BARATARIA BLVD MARRERO, LA

Michigan

Counterpoint Crisis Shelter   1-866-672-4357
715 Inkster Rd. Inkster, MI 48141
Two-week runaway and homeless shelter for individual youths aged 10-17.

Covenant House Michigan   (313)463-2000
2959 Luther King Jr. Blvd. Detroit, MI 48208
Emergency Shelter Tenns only

 DRMM Detroit Rescue Mission   (313)993-4700
3535 Third St. Detroit, MI 48231
Emergency Shelter Men Only

Delta County Alliance Against Violence & Abuse   (906)789-9207
140 N. 26th Street Escanaba, MI 49829
Emergency Shelter Domestic Violence Victims Only

Diane Peppler Resource   (906)635-0566
620 E Portage Ave Sault Ste. Marie, MI 49783
Victims of Domestic Violence are eligible. The Diane

Dwelling Place of Grand Rapids - Liz's House   (616)454-9390
343 S. Division Grand Rapids, MI 49503
Women and their Children Only

Dwelling Place of Grand Rapids - My Sisters House   (616)235-0223
761 Bridge Street NW Grand Rapids, MI 49504   Women Only

Eastside Emergency Center   (313)824-3060
5075 Chalmers Street Detroit, MI 48213
Emergency Shelter Transitional Housing - Family

Eaton County Shelter Program   (517)543-7350
240 S. Cochran Charlotte, MI 48813
Meals Clothing Must be 18+ years old if unaccompanied by parent

EightCAP Inc. Ionia/Montcaml Domestic Violence Program
(616)527-3351
413 West Main Street Ionia, MI 48846   Emergency Shelter

Emergency Shelter Services   (269) 925-1131
645 Pipestone Benton Harbor, MI 49022
Homeless families and single women

Emergency Shelter Services Inc.   (616)925-1131
645 Pipestone Street Benton Harbor, MI 49022
Emergency Shelter Women/Families with Children

Every Woman's Place   (231)759-7909
1221 West Laketon Avenue Muskegon, MI 49441
Domestic Violence Victims Only

Ezra House   (231)237-1111
106 Mason Street Charlevoix, MI 49720   Emergency Shelter

Family Counseling & Children's Services   (517)264-5733
220 North Main St. Adrian, MI 49221
Days Only Families/Singles

Family Counseling and Shelter   (734)241-0180
14390 Laplaisance Road Suite 106 Monroe, MI 48161
Emergency Shelter Direct Domestic Viloence Services

Friendship Shelter   (989)732-5960
7163 Old 27 S Gaylord, MI 49735

Emergency Shelter Must be 18+ years old if unaccompanied by parent

GENESIS ONE TRANSITIONAL YOUTH CENTER   313 459-4168
14353 EAST CANFIELD STREET DETROIT, MI 48224
SHELTER FOR HOMRLESS YOUTH RANGING FROM 8-24

Gla

ss House   (517)482-2028
419 N. Martin Luther King Blvd. Lansing, MI 48915
Emergency Shelter Women Only
 Good Samaritan House   (906)293-3180
314 Truman Boulevard Newberry, MI 49868
Emergency Shelter

Goodwill Inn   (231)922-4890
1329 South Division Street Traverse City, MI 49684
Emergency Shelter

Grace Centers of Hope   (231)334-2187
35 E. Huron Street Pontiac, MI 48342
Night Only Emergency Shelter

Grace Haven Center   (517)782-2980
1040 Francis Street Jackson, MI 49203   Emergency Shelter

Guiding Light Mission for Men   (616)451-0236
255 South Division Grand Rapids, MI 49503
Days Only Men Only

Haven House   (517)337-2731
121 Whitehills Drive East Lansing, MI 48823
Emergency Shelter Families Only

Haven of Rest Rescue Mission   (269)965-1148
148 East Michigan Battle Creek, MI 49017

Haven of Rest Rescue Mission   (269)965-1148
148 East Michigan Battle Creek, MI 49017   Emergency Shelter

Hispanic Center of Western Michigan   (616)742-0200
730 Grandville Ave S W Grand Rapids, MI 49503
Days Only Referrals Advocacy
 Holland Rescue Mission   (616)396-2200
356 Fairbanks Avenue Holland, MI 49423
Emergency Shelter Families/Singles

Housing Resources Inc.   (269)382-0287
345 N. Burdick St. Kalamazoo, MI 49007
Emergency Shelter Families Only

Iccf Family Haven   (616)247-4949
701 Prospect Avenue SE Grand Rapids, MI 49503
Families Only. The shelter will only accept men with families. Also,
women with children and families only.

Inasmuch House Haven of Rest   (269)965-1148
27 Green Street Battle Creek, MI 49017
Emergency Shelter

Inasmuch House Haven of Rest   (269)965-1148
27 Green Street Battle Creek, MI 49017

Inner City Christian Federation   (616)336-9333
816 Madison Ave.SE Grand Rapids, MI 49507
Emergency Shelter

Jackson Interfaith Shelter   (517)789-8735

414 S. Blackstone Jackson, MI 49201   Meals

Juvenile Division Program & Runaway Service of Jackson County
(517)788-4240
210 W. Mason Jackson, MI 49201
Emergency Shelter Teens only

Kalamazoo County Emergency Overnight Shelter   (269)388-3680
440-1/2 North Church Street Kalamazoo, MI 49007
Emergency Shelter

Kalamazoo Gospel Mission   (269)345-2974
448 N. Burdick Street Kalamazoo, MI 49007
Emergency Shelter Families/Singles

Loaves and Fishes Overnight Shelter   (517)482-2099
831 N. Sycamore Street Lansing, MI 48906
Emergency Shelter Families/Singles

Muskegon Rescue Mission   (616)727-6090
1691 Peck Street Muskegon, MI 49441
Emergency Shelter Families/Singles Separate men's and
women/family shelter programsl

Nehemiah Project   (231)347-0363
36 Bridge St. Petoskey, MI 49770
Night Only Emergency Shelter

Nehemiah Project
36 Bridge str. Petoskey , MI 49770

New Hope Shelter   (231)775-3702
814 Lynn Street Cadillac, MI 49601
Meals Clothing Accepts single men and families

Next Doo   (269)349-2119
1215/1217 W. North Street Kalamazoo, MI 49006
Emergency Shelter Women Only

Northwestern Michigan Human Services Agency   (231)47-3780
3963 Three Mile Road Traverse City, MI 49684
Days Only Families/Singles

OLHSA Livingston Human Service Agency   (517)546-8500
2300 E. Grand River Avenue Suite 107 Howell, MI 48843
Referrals Housing Services Advocacy

Oasis Shelter and Family Resource Center   (231)775-7299
601 Chestnut Street Cadillac, MI 49601
Emergency Shelter

Operation Get Down   (313)921-9422
10100 Harper Avenue Detroit, MI 48213
Transitional Housing - Family

Oscoda Full Gospel Comm. Church Shelter   (989)739-0019
115 First Street Oscode, MI 48750
Emergency Shelter

R.E.A.C.H. Runaway Program   (810)233-8700
914 Church Street Flint, MI 48502

North Carolina Homeless Shelters
Bethesda Center for the Homeless   (336)722-9951
930 N Patterson Avenue Winston Salem, NC 27101
Emergency Shelter Days Only

Catherine H. Barber Memorial Shelter Inc.   (336)838-7120

86 Sparta Road, North Wilkesboro, NC 28659
An overnight shelter with a place to wash clothes and bathe.

Charity Temple Ministry - The Children's Place   (252)345-1004
1834 Nc Highway 305 Aulander, NC 27805
Emergency Shelter Housing Placement Services

Charlotte Emergency Housing   (704)335-5488
2410 The Plz Charlotte, NC 28205
Emergency Shelter

Christians United Outreach Center   (336)625-1500
135 Sunset Ave. Asheboro, NC 27203
Days Only Emergency Shelter

Coastal Women's Shelter   (919)638-4509
1333 S. Glenburnie Road New Bern, NC 28561   Women's Shelter

Durham Rescue Mission   (919) 688-9641
1201 E. Main Street Durham, NC 27701   Food Sup

Edna McLaurin Transintonal Housing   (910) 822-2040

Pennsylvania
BEDFORD Human Services Administrator   (814)623-2002
10241 Lincoln Highway Everette, PA 15537
This is not a homeless shelter, This is an area homeless resource. If
you are in the area of BEDFORD Human Services Administrator,
call them for help regarding their Homeless Assistance Programs.

BERKS Human Services Coordinator - County Services Center
19601
633 Court Street, 13th Fl Reading, PA 19601

This is not a homeless shelter, This is an area homeless resource. If you are in the area of BERKS - Human Services Coordinator, call them for help regarding their Homeless Assistance Programs. Reading Shelters

BLAIR Blair County Human Services Office   (814)693-3112
423 Allegheny Street, Suite 443 Hollidaysburg, PA 16648-2022
This is not a homeless shelter, This is an area homeless resource. If you are in the area of BLAIR Blair County Human Services Office, call them for help regarding their Homeless Assistance Programs. Hollidaysburg Shelters

BRADFORD Bradford County Human Services
220 Main Street, Unit One Towanda, PA (570)265-1760
This is not a homeless shelter, This is an area homeless resource. If you are in the area of BRADFORD Bradford County Human Services, call them for help regarding their Homeless Assistance Programs.

BUCKS Bucks County Opportunity Council   Administration Office, 100 Doyle Street Doylestown, PA 18901(215)345-8
This is not a homeless shelter, This is an area homeless resource. If you are in the area of BUCKS Bucks County Opportunity Council, call them for help regarding their Homeless Assistance Programs.

BUTLER Community Action Program   (724)284-5125
P.O. Box 1208 Butler, PA 16003-1208
This is not a homeless shelter, This is an area homeless resource. If you are in the area of BUTLER Community Action Program, call them for help regarding their Homeless Assistance Programs.

Bell Socialization Services Inc.   (717)848-5767
160 South George Street York, PA 17401

Emergency Shelter Family Only

Bethesda Mission Men's Shelter   (717)257-4442
611 Reilly Street Harrisburg, PA 17102 Emergency Shelter Men

Florida

Central Care Mission   (407)299-6146
4027 Lennox Blvd Orlando, FL 32811

Christian Service Center of Central Florida   (407)425-2523
808 W Central Blvd Orlando, FL 32805

Coalition for the Homeless of Central Florida   (407)426-1250
639 W Central Blvd Orlando, FL 32801

Orlando Union Rescue Mission Men's Division   (407)423-3596
410 W Central Blvd Orlando, FL 32801

Salvation Army   (407)423-8581
400 W Colonial Dr Orlando, FL 32804

Salvation Army Men's Shelter   (407)423-8581
624 Lexington Ave Orlando, FL 32801

Women's residential Counseling Center   (407)425-2502
107 E Hillcrest St Orlando, FL 32801

New York

Bethel Gospel Assembly Shelter(c/o Bethel Gospel Assembly)
(212)860-1510   2-26 East 120th Street NY, NY 10037

Bowery Mission   (212)674-3456
227 Bowery NY, NY 10002

Grand Central Neighborhood Social Services Corporation (GCNSSC)
(212)818-1220
152 E. 44th Street NY, NY 10017

Harlem United Community AIDS Center   (212)531-1300
123-125 W 124th Street NY, NY 10027

Holy Apostles Soup Kitchen   (212)924-0167
296 9th Avenue NY, NY 10001

Homes for the Homeless   (212)529-5252
36 Cooper Square 6th Floor NY, NY 10003

Lutheran Family/Community Service   (212)265-1826
308 West 46TH Street NY, NY 10036

New York City Rescue Mission   (212)226-6214
90 Lafayette Street NY, NY 10013

Shelter and Food for the Homeless Inc.   (212)228-5254
602 E 9th Street NY, NY 10009
 St. Paul's House   (212)265-5433
335 West 51st Street NY, NY 10019

 American Rescue Workers   (207)777-1212391 Lisbon Street
Lisbon, ME 04240

Maine
Bread of Life Shelter   207-626-3479
157 Hospital Street Augusta, ME 04330
Family of domestic violence. Also single men and women's

Breakwater Teen Shelter   207-596-5793

218 Main Street Rockland, ME 04841   Homeless teen shelter.

Emmaus Center   207-667-3962

P.O. Box 811 Ellsworth, ME 04605   Temporary homeless shelter for all.

HOME, INC. - St. Francis Inn   207-469-6771

P.O. Box 223 East Orland, ME 04431

Homeless women's and family temporary shelter.

Harwich Ecumenical Council for the Homeless

PO Box 324 West Harwich, ME 02671

Hope Haven Gospel Mission   (207)783-6086

209 Lincoln Street Lewiston, ME 04240

Provides temporary shelter for all. Meals provided and is open 365 days a yr

Mid-Maine Homeless Shelter   207-872-6550

28 Ticonic Street Waterville, ME 04903

Homeless shelter that provides shelter for all. Also provides breakfast, dinner, showers, laundry facilities.

My Choice   1-800-773-9595

181 State Street Bangor, ME 04401

Housing for women with children or pregnant women.

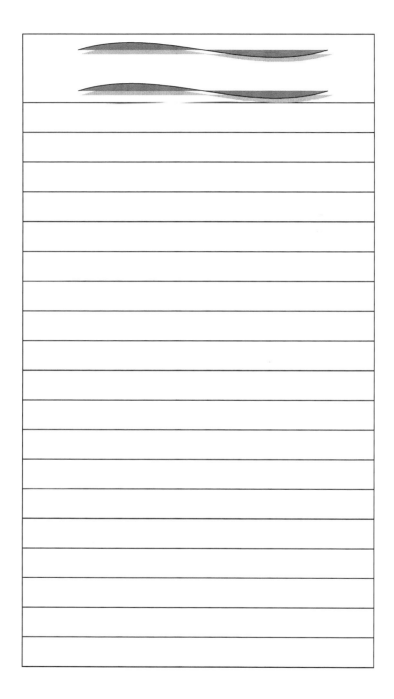

Works Cited

Kurtz, J. (n.d.). *The Arizona Republic.* Retrieved October 2009

MCSO. (2008, August 3). *Arpio and inmates celebrate 15 years.* Retrieved October 2009, from http\\www.msco.org\inmates

Unanamous. (2009, September 18). *Yahoo! Local.* Retrieved October 2009

Worker, S. J. (n.d.). *Job Services, Phoenix, Arizona.* Retrieved ctober 2009, from http://www.sjwjobs.org/index.html

(2009, March 6). Retrieved September 2009, from Mail Foreign Service.

Ehrenreich, B. (2009, August 9). *Divided Nation "This Landis Their Land".* Retrieved September 2009

Homeless, N. C. *Fact sheet #1.*

HomelessAmerca.com. (n.d.).

Jensen, D. (2006, December 13). *Funeral of murdered homeless man.* Retrieved October 5, 2009, from .

Lacey Peterson. (2009, September 1). *The Union Democrat.* Retrieved October 4, 2009

Lee, M. (2009, August 10). *Hate Crimes Report-08.* Retrieved October 2, 2009

Lowe, D. A. *Why shouldn't we have homeless children in Amerca.* Juneau Empire.

nationalhomeless.org. (n.d.).

Peyser, A. (n.d.). *American Girl's Homeless Doll.* Retrieved October 2009, 2009, from NY Post.

picture. *flicker.com.*

Press, A. (2007, 16 November). *Hurricane Katrina.* Retrieved October 5, 2009, from www.foxnews.com

Priddy, B. (2003, May 22). *County-paid death arrangements increasing in Down Economy.* Retrieved October 5, 2009, from http:||wwwmissouri,net

Foundation, F. S. (n.d.). *Fresh Start Woman's Foundation.* Retrieved October 2009, from http://www.wehelpwomen.com/default.aspx

Kurtz, J. (n.d.). *The Arizona Republic.* Retrieved October 2009

MCSO. (2008, August 3). *Arpio and inmates celebrate 15 years.* Retrieved October 2009, from http\\www.msco.org\inmates

Unanamous. (2009, September 18). *Yahoo! Local.* Retrieved October 2009

Worker, S. J. (n.d.). *Job Services, Phoenix, Arizona.* Retrieved ctober 2009, from http://www.sjwjobs.org/index.html

Thompson, P. (2009). *Pictured.* Retrieved 2009, from www.dailymail.co.uk.

Thompson, P. (2009, March 6). *the credit crunch tent city which has return ed to haunt america.* Retrieved SEP 2009

Tyler, R. (2009). *The NewsHour Extra.* Retrieved October 2009

unnomunous. (n.d.). Retrieved oct. 2, 2009

Made in the USA
Middletown, DE
24 February 2023

25354023R00139